THE HISTORY OF LLANTRISANT

DILLWYN LEWIS
Headmaster, Maesybryn County Primary School, Llantwit Fardre

Published by
DILLWYN LEWIS, Esq.
12 Llantrisant Road,
Beddau. Pontypridd
Mid Glamorgan
CF38 2BB

1966 Published by Author as Booklet

1975 First Edition, New and Revised

1982 Second Edition

ISBN 0 950056 73 1

Printed by
THE STARLING PRESS LTD.
RISCA, NEWPORT, GWENT NP1 6YB

Contents

To my Parents—Ann Maria Lewis and William John Lewis in gratitude for their affection, courage and self-sacrifice.

Foreword

by Sir Cennydd Traherne KG, TD
Lord-Lieutenant of the Counties of Glamorgan.
Freeman of Llantrisant

I am very glad to know of the New and Revised Edition of Mr. Dillwyn Lewis' book, The History of Llantrisant, first published in 1966 as a booklet.

The population of the Parish has greatly increased since then and there must be many residents who are unaware of its most interesting history. The pattern of Local Government has also radically changed recently but the name Llantrisant is still preserved in Church and Parish, Freemen and Town Trust.

Mr. Lewis' book will be a delight to new-comers and a refreshment to all who love this ancient place.

Llantrisant in 1893

Acknowledgements

The author acknowledges the assistance of Sir Cennydd Traherne K.G., T.D., Lord Lieutenant of the Counties of Glamorgan; Lieutenant-Colonel J. R. L. Traherne, Castellau Fawr; the Mayor and Taff-Ely Borough Council; Mid-Glamorgan County Council; Llantrisant Community Council; Llantrisant Town Trust; The Glamorgan Record Office; District Education Officer, W. B. Jones, B.A., Pontypridd; National Library of Wales; Ogwr Health Council; The Royal Mint; Aero Pictorial Ltd.; Tempest Ltd.; Celtic Press Ltd.; Western Mail and Echo Ltd.; Curator, Lambeth Palace, London; Miss Penelopen Price East Caerlan, Llantrisant; Miss Elspeth Rhys-Williams, Miskin Manor; Dewi P. Jones, Ph.C., M.P.S.; Rev. R. M. Owen, Vicar of Pontyclun; Rev. E. I. Davies, Vicar of Llantrisant; E. L. J. Smail, Esq., Glamorgan Hematitic Iron Ore Co. Ltd., Llanharry; David Glyn Lewis, B.A.; Edward Yendall, Esq.; H. Withers, Esq.; T. Hylton Warner, Esq.; D. Coghlan, Esq. for quotations from his collected notes on Court Leet and Vestry records; Rev. M. R. Ellis, B.A., for contributing " Bells of Llantrisant "; County Alderman William John Lewis, J.P. (Gwilym Llaeron) for his poems " Llantrisant Church " and "Ardal Castellau "; A print, Llantrisant in 1830, from " South Wales Illustrated " by Henry Gastineau; William Richards, A.R.P.S.; Martin Astrand, Esq.

Furthermore, the author wishes to record his most grateful thanks and appreciation for the encouragement of everyone and to all those who so generously tendered information and submitted photographs for inclusion in this book.

D.L.

Introduction

The Llantrisant Community Council came into being on the 1st April, 1974 on the reorganisation of Local Government in Wales. The former Parish Council had previously administered the same district since 1894, an area comprising Beddau, Llantrisant, Talbot Green, Penycoedcae, Groesfaen, Miskin, Talygarn and Pontyclun in the Town Ward and the Wards of Tonyrefail and Gilfach Goch.

Ever mindful of the historic importance of the Ancient Town of Llantrisant, once a Chartered Borough, but now part of the larger Borough of Taff-Ely, the town continues to make an important contribution to the economic and industrial environment of South Wales.

It gives me great pleasure and a sense of civic pride as Chairman of the Llantrisant Community Council to associate myself with the "History of Llantrisant" and to commend the book to all who live here and to visitors so that they, too, may know of our eventful past, busy present and hopeful future.

DOREEN POWELL,
Chairman of the Council.

Preface

As a Freeman and resident of Llantrisant, it gives me great pleasure to write this Preface to Dillwyn Lewis' book, which is a veritable treasure chest of information about a town which, in my opinion, is unique. Waves of development have washed round and by Llantrisant yet, it has somehow remained apart and defiantly different. From being the northern frontier of settled agricultural land, Llantrisant became the southern frontier of the booming South Wales coalfield. At its feet it has seen railways and new roads and most recently, spreading modern housing estates and superstores.

Llantrisant has retained its traditions and character that go back, in part, to the Norman and even pre-Norman eras. It has developed slowly, adapting to new developments without being overwhelmed by them. Less people come to shop or work in old Llantrisant but more are coming to enjoy the town. I hope that over the next few years, Llantrisant will come into its own as a tourist attraction, as somewhere local to have a pleasant walk, see a play or have a quiet drink. Few towns in South Wales can have the opportunities now presented to Llantrisant.

This book will, I am sure, be read by many visitors to Llantrisant providing each of them with a background to the town's rich heritage and traditions.

I wish it all the success the first edition had.

COUNCILLOR GEORGE PRESTON,
Mayor of Taff-Ely Borough Council.

Ordnance Survey Map of Beddau and District, published 1883
(Crown Copyright)

Author's Note

The controversial history of Llantrisant has always been of great interest and aroused much curiosity. This was renewed with even greater enthusiasm when, during December 1964, an exhibition entitled "Presenting the Parish to the Parish" which I helped to arrange in co-operation with Rev. Malcolm Ellis, B.A., to mark the coming of age of the Youth Movement within the Church in Wales, took place. It told the story of Llantrisant Parish in pictures and other interesting objects including several belonging to Dr. William Price. The exhibition was opened by Miss Penelopen Price, the daughter of Dr. Price, founder of Modern Cremation. Photographic items seen at this exhibition have been included to illustrate this book.

During the past ten years since the booklet version of this history, the Llantrisant district has developed beyond recognition. After many years of solitude, the town has become the centre of social and industrial interest. The establishment of a new town here continues to be debated.

The communities in all parts of the district continue to flourish and grow, bringing new groups like the Civic Society, formed to improve the amenities. The Llantrisant Town skyline has been radically changed.

Two new Industrial Estates have been established and the Royal Mint has moved here from its historic site near the Tower of London. History was made by the fact that coins for the New Decimal Coinage of 1971 were made at Llantrisant.

Comprehensive Education was established in September 1972 at the newly-built Bryn Celynnog Comprehensive School at Beddau.

With the Reorganisation of Local Government on 1st April 1974, the Llantrisant district was merged with the Urban District of Pontypridd forming the new administrative area of Taff-Ely which has been granted Borough Status. Thus the wheel of time has turned full circle and Llantrisant enjoys once more the honour of being a Borough within the new larger area administered by the Mid-Glamorgan County Council.

DILLWYN LEWIS

Aerial View of Llantrisant by Tempest, Cardiff

1. Llantrisant – A Welsh Hill Town

The town of Llantrisant is the oldest town in the Ely Valley. Its former title was the "Ancient Borough of Llantrisant." "Llantrisant is built on the brow of a hill, commanding beautiful and extensive views of the Vale of Glamorgan. The magnificent view is ample recompense for the ascent through the steep winding streets of Llantrisant to where stand the church and castle. The streets still retain traces of the age of the town as they are paved with cobbles in the old-fashioned way".

The word 'Llantrisant' literally means the 'Church of Three Saints'. The church is dedicated to the Saints: Illtyd, Gwynno and Tyfodwg.

A practice which dated from the remote ages was that of whitening the houses. Even the walls of yards and gardens were whitened. This custom was noticed and praised in the most ancient Welsh poems. A very ancient poem, attributed to Aneurin who lived about the year 550 states:—

> "*In Glamorgan the people are courteous and gentle,*
> *Married women are honoured, and the walls are white.*"

Dafydd ap Gwilym, a bard living about 1350 says of Glamorgan:—

> "*The bard loves this beautiful country,*
> *Its wines and its white houses.*"

And in another place:—

> "*Thou sunning morning, beam joyfulness around,*
> *And salute the white houses of Glamorgan.*"

In the vicinity of Llantrisant, the names of the farmhouses seem to correspond to the importance of the place in time of war, such as "Gad-y-Meirch", "Gelli fuddgar" or "Gelli-beddau'r-gaer". Two miles north-east of Llantrisant there is a new and growing village called Beddau (graves). It is said that many soldiers were killed in a fierce battle, which occurred in the area and the bodies were buried, where the village now stands. A short distance north of the town is a small rural district called Castellau which means fortifications. The mansion has the appearance of having at one time occupied a position of note. It is situated on the side of the old road which was made by Gwrgan, one of the old princes of Glamorgan. The road led from Llantwit Major the educational centre, to Hirwaun (Wurgan) near Aberdare. In 1630, the mansion was occupied by Edmund Traherne, Esq., Portreeve of Llantrisant at that time. To the east of the town is Caerau, which is situated on a prominent hill. These are earthworks of a hill fort of considerable extent and are well preserved. They are nearly circular in form, and composed of earth and stones with triple defences—three banks and two ditches—on one side. At Rhiwsaeson, which is south of Llantrisant, a severe battle was fought in 873 between the Danes and Saxons.

Llantrisant, until 1883, boasted the importance of being a Corporate Town; created such by a Charter granted by Hugh de Spencer in 1346. This Charter, which is still in existence, was confirmed by a later one, bearing the date 20th October, 1424. It grants the Freemen as Burgesses, certain privileges in the town, and properties known as the 'Cymdda' or Common and the Graig, comprising about 284 acres, are put under their jurisdiction. In 1883, the Municipal Corporations Act was passed by Parliament. The act gave authority to abolish certain corporations one of which was Llantrisant. By this time, the market at Llantrisant had declined in favour of Pontypridd. The records of the Court Leet show that the administration of the borough was inefficient. An item for 30th September, 1785 states "that many records of this Court Leet have been lost". In May, 1847, "The Jurors present that the Halberts belonging to the Corporation should be sought after and that the Constables of the Court should use their best endeavours to recover them. The weights and measures having been found they present that the Portreeve should furnish proper scales for the use of the Corporation". This indifferent attitude caused Llantrisant to lose its charter. The properties are now administered by the Llantrisant Town Trust established by order of the Charity Commissioners of England and Wales on 17th December, 1889.

A quotation from documents in the Public Record Office relating to the period 1262-1280 states "That a terrible conflict took place between the men of Glamorgan and the Normans. In that fight in the streets of Llantrisant, 100 houses were destroyed in the town" and "destruction of the Wind Mill near the town" is mentioned. The record shows that Llantrisant was important during this period. Leland during his famous itinerary came to Llantrisant about 1540. He describes the castle. "The Castelle on the toppe of the hille and ys in ruine. It has been a fair castelle and 2 wardes, and the inner diked having among other towers one great and high caulled Giguran (Gigfran-Raven), and at this Castelle is the prison for Miskin and Glin Rodiney". Leland also states that ironworks were in existence when he visited the town. The town now gets it wealth chiefly from the tinplate works, collieries and brickworks in the district.

More recent itinerants had visited Llantrisant and recorded their impressions. Several of the records relate to the nineteenth century. B. H. Malkin in his "Anquities of South Wales" 1807 states:—

> *"Llantrisant in its intercourse with the Vale is very limited and irregular, and though a town not of very small population, the appearance of a stranger excites some curiosity and surprise. The houses, with the exception of two or three, are in a style very inferior in point of comfort to those in Welsh towns, especially near the sea."*

Henry Skrine in his "Tours through Wales", in 1811 said of this town:—

> "*Llantrisant with its whitened buildings which appear like a swarm of bees. The streets, of course, are steep and narrow. A good road is lately carried hence to Pontypridd.*"

Thomas Rees in "The Beauties of England and Wales" in 1815 records that:—

> "*Llantrisant has little else (other than its fine view overlooking Glamorgan) to recommend attention. It contains a few respectable private dwellings, but the generality of the houses are very indifferent. The remains of the castle are very scanty.*"

Since 1894, when Parliament passed an Act relating to Local Government, the administration, management, and control of the Town and district, has been vested in a new body known as the Rural District Council which is the authority for Paths, Sanitary and other purposes, with limited urban powers. The Llantrisant and Llantwit Fardre Rural Parishes were joined together and formed a district called "Llantrisant and Llantwit Fardre Rural District Council". The district is composed of three Wards: Town Ward, Tonyrefail and Llantwit Fardre. A fourth Ward, Gilfach Goch, was made in 1919. Since Local Government Reorganisation on 1st April 1974, the four wards now form part of the Borough of Taff-Ely.

The "freemen" of the borough, however, still hold a Court Leet in the town-hall. Two meetings of the Court are held each year, one in May and the other in December. At both of the meetings "Freemen" are enrolled. In 1946, during the victory celebrations of the 1939-45 war, the Court Leet revived the old custom of perambulating the boundaries of the old town. Another revival was the formation of an Archery Club at Llantrisant. This was inaugurated during 1951. The reason for the interest in archery is that during the French War in 1346, a legion was formed by the Lord of Glamorgan to assist Edward III in France; and at the Battle of Crècy some members of the legion were natives of Llantrisant, fought with great valour. At this battle, the Black Prince (Prince of Wales) took the blind King John of Bohemia prisoner. The Crest and Motto of King John was three ostrich feathers with the words "Ich Dean" (I Serve), and this has since been borne by successive Princes of Wales as their Crest and Motto. Because of this connection with the Black Prince, the people of Llantrisant are often called the 'Black Army' whenever a quarrel arises between a resident of the old town and some of the neighbouring villages.

Llantrisant is also famous as the home of modern cremation, for in the year 1884 a local doctor, William Price, rather crudely attempted to cremate the body of his child. He was tried at the Cardiff Assizes, where the case was dismissed on payment of one farthing costs. Dr. Price died in 1893 and was himself cremated at East Caerlan, Llantrisant. It was the first public cremation in the country. In September 1947 a brass tablet was unveiled at Llantrisant by Miss Penelopen Price, under the auspices of the National Cremation Society. Miss Price was Dr. Price's daughter and taught music at Llantrisant, where she resided. Llantrisant also has connections with the forebears of Oliver Cromwell, who were natives of the parish, as also was Sir Leoline Jenkins, Secretary of State under Charles II.

2. Llantrisant Castle

The scanty ruins of tne castle are situated on good elevation, commanding extensive views of the surrounding country and stand in the centre of the town near the church. It has the appearance of once occupying a formidable position of defence. Now, only a portion of a tower remains to attract the attention of visitors and is greatly neglected. The site is now a public recreation ground.

The castle is of great antiquity and its origin is ascribed to different dates. In the time of Edward I, the castle was in the possession of Gilbert de Clare (Red Lord of Glamorgan) who did homage to Edward on his accession to the titles and estates of his family after the death of his father. Rice Meyrick in his book of Glamorgan Antiquities (1578) mentions: —

> " *It is said that Earl Galfridus Monemutensis built the castle of Llantrisant in the time Sir Robert Morris was Sheriffe of Glamorgan.*"

G. T. Clark in his " Land of Morgan " refers to Llantrisant castle and mentions: —

> " *Earl Robert seems to have built a castle at Llantrisant and the accounts of the lordship in* 1184 *shows that the castles of Newport, Kenfig and Neath were at that time regularly established fortresses.*"

Llantrisant castle is reported to have been " second only to Cardiff in military importance ".

The Lordship of Glamorgan, after the death of Fitzhamon passed to Robert (Consul), Earl of Gloucester, who was a natural son of Henry I. He married Mabel, daughter of Fitzhamon and from her descendants the Lordship came by marriage to the de Clares, Earls of Gloucester and Hertford; then to the de Spencers, Beauchamps and Nevills successively.

Many castles were in use in Glamorgan but there is no certainty for how long a period Llantrisant castle was used as a residence. Records state that in 1252, a daughter was born to the Earl of Gloucester at Llantrisant. She was christened Margaret. In 1263, Earl Gilbert de Clare did homage and had livery of the castles of Llantrisant and Cardiff. Writs were issued in 1297, to Walter de Hacklut, custos to complete the gate of the castle of Llantrisant which he had begun.

By the time of the death of Gilbert de Clare (the red Lord) in 1295, the lordships of Senghenydd, Miscyn and Glynrhondda had all come into the immediate possession of the Lord of Glamorgan and were administered by his officers; but they still retained their seperate courts and, it seems, their old Welsh laws and customs. The Lordship was held by four de Clares: —

(1) Gilbert (1217-1230)
(2) Richard (1230-1262)
(3) Gilbert the Red (1262-1295)
(4) Gilbert (died gallantly at Bannockburn in 1314) (1307-14).

On the death of Earl Gilbert in 1314, the earl's executors had a writ to give seizen to the heirs. Bartholomew de Badlesmere was in charge of Glamorgan and all officers of the lordship were to have the same fees as in the time of the Earl, 'also he is to store the castle'. The fees to the constable of Llantrisant castle were I13 : 6 8d. In 1315, William Fleming as Bailiff was given the custody of the Castle and the forest of Miskin. Afterwards he incurred the king's displeasure and was executed in Cardiff for treason. In May 1317, the castle had a 'Receiver of Stores and Garnisture' at a wage of I5 a year. He was responsible for munitioning the castle with food and other necessities, a duty of the Constable.

By 1317, the de Spencers had succeeded as Lords of Glamorgan. There were four Lords:

(1) Hugh, the younger (1317-1326)
(2) Hugh, his son (1338-1349)
(3) Edward le Despenser (1349-1375)
(4) Thomas le Despenser (1375-1400).

The castle was of little account from 1404. It is not certain whether the castle was demolished or destroyed. It is known that Llewellyn Bren, a landowner on the left bank of the Taff in the hill country led a rebellion. He was Prince of Senghenydd and felt that he had been unjustly treated over the ownership of some land and had rebelled against the Lord of Glamorgan. The rebellion took place in 1316. It is also supposed that the castle was demolished by Owen Glyndwr in 1404, when he raided the county. Leland found it in ruin and described it as "a fair castelle with two wardes, the inner diked". The castle was circular in plan with a horse-shoe-shaped bailey. Its curtain walls must have been high, judging by the fragment of the drum tower, which remains to this day.

Llantrisant castle figured in the flight of Edward II from his queen, Isabella. There are many versions of the King's flight but what might be the truth is "that a Cistercian monk from Neath guided the party to the Cistercian monastic establishment at Penrhys (Rhondda Valley); that while there refreshing themselves before proceeding to Llantrisant castle, the monk found an opportunity of communicating with the spies; that the spies intercepted the party somewhere on the ancient highway leading from the Rhondda to Llantrisant". The spot where the King was captured is still called "Pant-y-Brad" (The Hollow of Treason). Hugh de Spencer was captured at Gwaunmiskin, East of Llantrisant, and "others of the King's company in the Park of Cloone, on the South part of the hill whereupon Llantrisant is builded." The King and his friends were then taken to Llantrisant castle. "David ap Meuric and his fellow-custodians of the castle may have been as much surprised as shocked when Henry of Lancaster knocked at the gate for admittance with his string of distinguished captives ". The constable at this time may have been Robert de Aston. He is referred to in 1327 as " sometimes constable of Lantrissen ", and was very active in that year as " taxor, collector and inquisitor ".

Edward II ended his reign in the land where his life began. Near Llantrisant was enacted the crowning tragedy of his reign. Many traditions of the royal fugitive are preserved with a jealous care. B. H. Malkin in his "Antiquities of South Wales " states: —

> " *It is said that the King in his own person was beloved by the Welsh, and would have been safe in his retirement at Llantrisant, had he not trusted himself to the monk in preference to their protection* ".

3. Llantrisant Church

The church stands a short distance from the castle but the exact date when the foundation of the first church was laid is not known. It is suggested that the Norman Church was built in the year 1096. In 1386 Llantrisant Church was under the jurisdiction of the Abbot of Tewkesbury. When Tewkesbury Abbey was dissolved in 1539, the living of Llantrisant came under the Dean and Chapter of Gloucester, who remained in charge until 1885. Since 1885, the Church of Llantrisant has been governed by the Bishops of Llandaff. The church is dedicated to the memory of three saints: Saint Illtyd, Saint Tyfodwg and Saint Gwynno. The building was originally of the Norman style of architecture, but very little of the original church now remains. The only traces of Norman architecture are the Font, a portion of the south door and the lower part of the western arch of the Nave. The tower is about 70 feet high and contains a peal of Six Bells (1718).

The present church was built by the Earl of Glamorgan, Hugh de Spencer and was restored in 1873. In 1894, the tower and the west end of the Nave were restored and the bells were re-hung and a white marble bapistery, for baptism by immersion, was placed under the tower. The church is styled " the Mother Church " which indicates that the church is of older foundation than the chapels dependent upon it. The living is a vicarage and two curacies come under the jurisdiction of the vicar.

While workmen were carrying out some excavations for the restoration of the tower, they made a unique discovery which turned out to be the mould for casting bells, as well as the furnace and other implements for casting. The pit, after use, had been filled in and forgotten. It is unusual that the Belfry of a church should have been used as a foundry.

Many of the decorations and ' movables ' are gifts to the church presented from time to time in memory of various persons. Three forms of lighting are exhibited in the church. A fine brass candelabra which was used before gas lighting was introduced, is still displayed in spite of the fact that electric light has been installed as a memorial to those who fell in the second world war. Two ' movables ' which have a special place in the treasures of the church are the Elizabethan styled chalice, which is still used during Communion services, and a silver Communion Plate, dated 10th October, 1750. They are described in " Llandaff Church Plate " by G. E. Halliday (1901) as :—

> " *A silver chalice No. 7 ins. in height with a paten cover hall-marked* 1626. *It resembles an Elizabethan cup circa* 1576 *in general design.*
>
> *A handsome bread-dish, hall-marked* 1750, *inscribed " The gift of William and Jane Mathews, Llantrisant, Oct.* 10*th* 1750 " *round which is engraved, " For we have seen His Star in the*

east and have come to worship Him". The dish is 11½ ins. in diameter, with an embossed edge, standing on three feet, 1½ ins. high.

A copper gift chalice No. 2 and paten, the gift of J. Coates Carter, Esq., 1897."

A new pulpit was presented by Miss Rosie Silkstone of Bury, in memory of her parents. It was designed by Mr. George Pace and dedicated on 18th June, 1967 by Dr. Glyn Simon, Archbishop of Wales.

The stained glass windows record the connection of the church with the Prichard family of Collena, Tonyrefail, and tablets line the walls in memory of the Hewett family of Tir-mab-Ellis.

The east window, dating from 1873, is the work of Morris Burne-Jones and represents Christ as unbearded. The church registers date from 1720. An effigy of a warrior has been placed in the wall of the church. It is said to represent Cadwgan Fawr of Miskin who was the son of Dydd ap Cynvrig Vychan, from Rhys Goch, ap Richard, ap Einon, ap Collwyn. He was a man of distinction and is supposed to have opposed Gilbert de Clare, when de Clare attempted to suppress Welsh customs. The most ancient monument in the church was a slab of stone with a roughly carved processional cross. This is supposed, from its character, to have commemorated some Ecclesiastical Dignitary and may suggest the remains of an earlier Celtic Church foundation.

In the churchyard are the graves of famous South Wales families, notably the Prichards of Collena, Tonyrefail, whose descendants are mentioned by B. H. Malkin in his book on South Wales:—

"*The aforesaid Prichards were descendants of Efan ap Prichard, ap Gibbon ap Llewellyn ap Ivor Hir of Miskin, ap Howell, ap Ivor Ychan, ap Ivor Hen, ap Caradog, ap Einon, ap Cadivor, ap Collwyn. It was a remarkable usage of the Welsh, derived from high antiquity, for the son to take the Christian name of his father for his own surname . . . a man named Evan, whose father's name was Richard, called himself Evan Prichard.*"

Since the reign of Henry VIII, Welshmen have adopted permanent family surnames, after the manner of the English. The Trumans of Llantrisant also rest in the Churchyard. The family descend from the Herberts of Pembroke and the Trumans of Northampton. Some members of the family still live in the district.

The old vicarage at Llantrisant was pulled down, after a new house had been built on an adjacent site. The old vicarage was a large house in extensive grounds and was built by Rev. Robert Rickards (1766-1810). It has served all incumbents from 1770 until 1966. In 1965 the vicarage and its lands were sold to a firm, which built a modern vicarage near the old vicarage gates, and developed the rest of the land into a housing estate known as Coed yr Esgob.

THE VICARS OF LLANTRISANT SINCE THE YEAR 1630

Rev. Richard Bassett.

Rev. Henry Williams (ejected from Llantrisant 1662).

Rev. Thomas Bassett.

Rev. John Lloyd.

Rev. Antonius Jones.

Rev. Edmund Walters.

Rev. John Loughor.

Rev. James Harries B.D., also Rector of Llanharry and Prebend of Llandaff d. 29th April. 1728.

Rev. Robert Rickards, d. 15th November, 1810.

Rev. James Morgan, D.D., d. 11th June, 1816.

Rev. William Michell, M.A., d. 15th February, 1829.

Rev. J. B. Williams, d. 23rd June, 1845.

Rev. Evan Morgan, d. 22nd November, 1864.

Rev. J. Powell Jones, B.D., d. 21st December, 1883.

Rev. Joshua Pritchard Hughes, consecrated Bishop of Llandaff 1905, Resigned 1931, d. 1938.

Rev. D. T. Griffiths, 1905-23.

Rev. D. H. Simon, 1923-32.

Rev. Wm. Percival Jones, 1932-36.

Rev. W. Sturdy, 1936-46.

Rev. J. J. Thomas, B.A., Vicar, 1946-56.

Rev. Edwin Isaac Davies, B.A., Vicar 1957-79.

Rev. Peter Lewis, B.A., Vicar since 1979.

4. The Bells of Llantrisant

The massive Tudor tower, which houses the bells of the Parish Church of Llantrisant is much later than the original Norman church, having been built c. 1490. Although there are indications that an earlier Mediaeval tower stood on the same spot, how much of it remains in the existing structure is difficult to assess. There were hung in this tower, soon after its completion, six bells, somewhat heavier than the present bells rung each Sunday. These bells were cast in a specially prepared workshop, directly underneath the tower, but we must not assume that they were made by local craftsmen, as some have been inclined to believe. It was a common practice for bell-founders to travel all over the country, carrying out their work where it was required in order to overcome the expense and other problems of transport.

Because of the state of the bells in 1718, they were transported (probably by way of the sea and rivers) to E. Evans of Chepstow where they were melted down, and a completely new set of six bells was cast. Unfortunately, they were not quite as heavy as the originals, but their tone was still considered to be very pleasing to the ear. Those same six bells form the basis of the present ring of eight, and bear the following inscriptions:—

Treble: PROSPERITY TO THOSE THAT LOVE GOOD BELLS, E.E. 1718.

Second: GLORIA DEO IN EXCELSIS, PAX IN TERRA, E.E. 1718. (Glory to God in the highest, peace on earth).

Third: ECCLESIA ANGLICANA, CONTRA POP: ET FANATICOS FLOREAT, 1718. (May the Church of England flourish against plunderers and fanatics).

Fourth: MORGAN DAVID, EVAN MORGAN, CHURCH WARDENS, E.E. 1718.

Fifth: JACOBUS HARRIES, SACER, THEOLOG: BACC: 1718. (James Harries, B.D., a holy man).
Recast by the firm of "Charles Carr" Bellfounders, 1893.

Tenor: RICHARDUS JENKINS DE HENSOL, ARMIGER, E.E. ANNO DOMINI 1718. (Richard Jenkins of Hensol, Captain).

The inscriptions on the first three bells suggest that the rigours of Cromwell's army, some sixty years earlier, had been felt in Llantrisant and still rankled in the memory of those who cherished the beauties of their Parish Church. This is quite understandable if (as is very probable) many of its treasures had been destroyed and even the bells damaged to such an extent as to necessitate such thorough renovation.

About 150 years later, not very long after John Pritchard's restoration of the main part of the Church had been completed, J. P. Seddon was entrusted with the task of further restoration of the Tower; and as the floor of the Tower was being excavated for the purpose of installing a Baptistry and a heating chamber, some interesting discoveries were made. The workmen found part of an old furnace and some of the foundry tools, which date back to the casting of the original bells. The furnace and a plaster-core of the original Tenor bell can still be seen today.

The structure of the Tower needed extensive repairs and while these were being carried out, the bells were lowered to be tuned and quarter-turned by the firm of Charles Carr of Smethwick. Quarter-turning is a process of rotating the bell, so that the clapper strikes the bell in a different spot. This work was done locally for the most part, but the Fifth, which had developed a crack, was taken away to be recast and fitted with a new head and clapper attachment. The old frame too, which was fixed solidly into the Tower wall was replaced by the present free-standing one, the advantage being that the effect of the swinging bells was partly transferred from the walls to the frame itself, thus considerably reducing the wear on the stonework.

The fifteenth-century arch between the Tower and the nave had at some time been entirely bricked up, but for a small doorway at ground level. This was removed to reveal not only the arch in all its glory, but also the beautiful, deeply recessed Tudor window, just above the West door, which is also one of the most pleasant interior views in the Church. When the bells were rehung in 1893, provision was made in the frame for two further bells to be added when money became available. The draught of rope was shortened and the ringers, who had previously operated from the bottom of the Tower, now rang on a new floor where they have rung ever since. Underneath was a space for a choir vestry. A robed choir was first introduced by Revd. Joshua Pritchard Hughes. Subsequently the choir vestry was enhanced by the erection of a fine oak screen to the memory of the late Canon John Powell Jones. The ringing order was also changed from anti-clockwise to the opposite direction. Before, the Treble had been rung roughly from the position where the Sixth is rung today, the Second from Fifth position, and so on.

Now we come to the last chapter in the story of the bells. Over thirty years passed before the plan for adding two more bells became a reality, and even then not entirely as at first envisaged. It had been intended to add a Seventh and a new Tenor, but this would have involved re-tuning most of the existing bells to obtain the correct intervals of the scale; by adding instead a Treble and Second, no tuning was necessary. At any rate this is what happened and the two bells were placed in position in 1926, after a slight modification to the frame had been made to take two small bells instead of two large ones. The adjustment can be clearly seen on examination. As a result we now have the rare instance of the Tenor hanging at the corner of the frame instead of in the centre. The new bells were made by " Taylor of Loughboro " and their inscriptions are:—

Treble:	TALIESIN MORGAN 1926.	
Second:	JOHN JOHN MALGWYN H. DAVIES	CHURCH WARDENS 1926.

A large photograph in the Parish Church records the occasion in which the bells were dedicated by Bishop Hughes on 4th December, 1926. The eight bells range in weight from about 1 cwt. to 12 cwt., and are in the key of F.

5. Charities of Llantrisant

(as listed in the Report to The House of Commons, 1897).

SIR LEOLINE JENKINS'S CHARITY

Sir Leoline Jenkins, by Will, dated shortly before the 1st day of September, 1685, charged all his lands and hereditaments, in the county of Glamorgan, which he devised to the principal fellows and scholars of Jesus College, Oxford, with the payment of the yearly sum of 100**l**.; and, after directing that 80**l**., part thereof, should be applied for the benefit of the free school at Cowbridge, he bequeathed 20**l**., the residue thereof, to the binding apprentices poor children born in the parishes of Llantrisant, Llanblithian, the town of Cowbridge, and the parish of Ystrad Owen, or the clothing old poor people of one of the said three parishes or town, at the discretion of the schoolmaster of the free school at Cowbridge, he first consulting the respective ministers thereof, but the determination being left to himself; and he directed that the said parishes and town should respectively receive the whole 20**l**. every fourth year, in the order aforesaid; and that the schoolmaster should give an account of what he should so order, year by year, to the principal of the aforesaid college; and the testator, after directing his executors to purchase the site of a chapel of ease, in the parish of Llantrisant, called Cappell Tal y garn, and to put the same in good repair, charged his aforesaid lands and hereditaments with the payment of 10**l**. a year, for ever, towards maintaining of divine service in the said chapel.

This charity has, since the year 1788, been very carefully administered according to the directions of the founder, by the Rev. Dr. Williams, the master of the free school at Cowbridge; and all the accounts relating to it have been kept by him with great regularity. The 20**l**. has been wholly expended, during that period, in the purchase of clothing; and each of the places named by the testator has received the entire benefit of that sum every fourth year. The clothes are distributed amongst poor old people, principally women, who are nominated by Dr. Williams, upon the recommendation of the respective ministers of the parishes and town entitled to participate in the charity; and the same persons are allowed to partake of it every fourth year, so long as they continue residents of the same place. Previous to each distribution, the list of the persons who partook of the previous one is sent to the minister of the parish to erase the names of those who may have died, and to recommend others in their stead. The clothes given away in Llantrisant consist of a cloth coat for the men, and a gown or petticoat of half-cloth for the women; and the number of persons amongst whom they are distributed generally amounts to about 30, of whom, on an average, 25 are women. The last distribution of the charity, in this parish, was made in 1835.

The 10**l**. a year bequeathed by the testator for maintaining divine service in the chapel of ease which he directed to be purchased, is regularly paid by the principal of Jesus College, Oxford, to the minister of that chapel.

The income of this Charity is now devoted to the purchase of blankets, which are distributed by the vicar. The number of blankets vary, but about 20 poor persons receive one or two blankets apiece at each distribution.

The head-master of Cowbridge School, being the incumbent of Talygarn Chapel, purchases the blankets, and sometimes recommends one or two poor persons of the village of Brynsadler as fitting persons to receive the Charity, but takes no further part in the administration. Poor people in receipt of parish relief are not excluded from the list. The distribution in this parish took place this year.

The Rev. W. F. Evans, incumbent of Talygarn Chapel, regularly receives the sum of 10*l*. a year for holding divine service at Talygarn every Sunday afternoon. The old chapel is now a ruin, but a very beautiful church has been built adjoining it by Mr. G. T. Clark, of Talygarn.

CATHERINE POWELL'S CHARITY

Catherine Powell, by Will, dated the 6th day of November, 1739, charged one moiety of a messuage and lands called Trebannog, in the parish of Llantrisant, which she devised to her nephew, Gervas Powell, in fee, with the expense of finding, and maintaining thereon for ever, one milch cow with summer and winter foddering and the changing thereof as occasion should require, for the use of seven poor people living next to her mansion house, at Milton, to be nominated by her grandson and his heirs; and she further charged the same tenement with seven half-crowns, to be paid at Candlemas, yearly, for ever, to such seven persons as should have the benefit of the said cow.

It would appear, by the Parliamentary Returns of 1786, that, up to that period, the benefit of this charity was received according to the intentions of the testatrix. For upwards of 40 years, however, it has been altogether discontinued; and it will be observed that it was originally void, under the statute 9 Geo. II., cap. 36.

Nothing was known of this Charity in 1897, beyond the fact that a stone tablet in St. John's Baptist Chapel at Tonyrefail records the gift.

It is worthy of note that, although in the Report of 1837 this Charity is included among the Charities of Llantrisant parish, the beneficiaries, i.e., " seven poor people living next her mansion house at Milton ", would be residents of the parish of Llancarvan, in which Milton is situate.

WILLIAM GIBBON'S CHARITY

William Gibbon, by Will, dated the 18th day of September, 1809, bequeathed the sum of 500*l*. to John Price and Richard Hoare Jenkins, their executors and administrators, upon trust, to invest the same in one of the public funds of Great Britain, in their names, or in the name of the survivor of them, his executors or administrators, and to execute a declaration to stand possessed of the stock so to be purchased, upon trust, to pay or permit the rector of the parish of Llanharry to receive the interest or dividends of 200l. part of the said sum of 500l., or of the said stock, to be distributed by him, on Christmas-day, yearly, among such of the industrious poor of good character, residing within the said parish of Llanharry, as to him should seem proper; and, as to the interest or dividends of 100l., other part of the said sum of 500l., or of the said stock, for the like poor of the parish of Llanharran, as aforesaid, at the like discretion of the rector of that parish; and, as to the interest or dividends of 100l., further part of the said sum of 500l., or of the said stock, for the like poor of the parish of Llantrissant, as aforesaid, at the like discretion of the vicar of that parish; and as to the sum of 100l., the residue of the said 500l., or of the said stock, for the like poor of the parish of Llanblethian, at the like discretion of the vicar of that parish.

ANNE GIBBON'S CHARITY

In the year 1826 Wyndham Lewis, Esq., the executor of Anne Gibbon, pursuant to her charitable bequest of 500l. to Llanharry, Llanblethian, Llantrisant and Llanharran, purchased therewith 825l. 6s. 6d. 3 per cent Consols. This Stock was, at the request of the personal representatives of Anne Gibbon, transferred on December 1st of that year to Richard Hoare Jenkins, of Llanharan House, who on December 9th entered into a declaration of trust with regard to it, believing it to be the interest arising from William Gibbon's bequest. The Stock was sold on 20th March, 1828, but acting upon the representations of " the Commissioners of 1837 for inquiries concerning Charities ", the like sum of 825l. 6s. 6d. Consols was purchased in the name of the said Richard Hoare Jenkins on 9th May, 1837.

The income derived from these two foundations is distributed together by the vicar and his curates, who find out the most needy persons in the different districts, and bestow on them sums varying from one shilling to half-a-crown. The distribution takes place soon after Christmas. The dividends are placed on deposit at a local bank as they are received by the vicar, and a few shillings are gained in this way from the interest accruing.

RICHARD HOWELL'S CHARITY

Richard Howell, by will dated 3rd November, 1856, proved at Llandaff 6th February, 1858 directed his trustees to invest 100l., free of legacy duty, in Government Stock in perpetuity to bear interest payable yearly, which should be laid out in the purchase of bread made of wheaten flour, to be divided in three equal portions between the poor in equal shares at Christmas annually, one-third to 20 poor persons residing in the town of Llantrisant, one other third to the like number of poor persons residing in the village of Llanharran, and the remaining one-third to the like number of poor persons residing in the village of Aberdare, and if it should happen that such number of poor persons should not be located in each of the several places named, then, and in each case the deficiency should be supplied by poor persons adjacent thereto.

This bequest owed its origin to a slander action in which Richard Howells, of Rhiwfelin, recovered 100**l**. as damages from William Williams, of Garth Hall. The interest on this amount was distributed by him in his lifetime to the poor, and by his will he directed that the interest should be divided yearly among the poor in the three parishes in which he was best known. The testator died 26th November, 1857.

The income arising from this endowment amounts to 1**l**. 1s. 4d. a year. The vicar does not consider that the distribution of a shilling to 20 poor persons would be of the slightest benefit, and he therefore places the dividends, as they are paid to him, on deposit account at a local bank, and they are allowed to accumulate until some period of exceptional distress. During the winter of 1849, 10**l**. 0s. 4d. was distributed among the poor, who were given tickets of the value of 5s. each, and allowed to buy what food they wished from the tradesmen in the town. Over 40 persons benefited, as private individuals subscribed a small amount in aid of this fund.

MISS LISLE'S CHARITY

Frances Anne Berkin Meackham Lisle, spinster, by Will dated 2nd March, 1875 (proved at the Principal Registry 31st January, 1877) directed a sufficient sum to be invested in the Consolidated 3**l** per cent. Annuities to produce the annual sum of 5**l**. (free of duty), and that the sum of 2**l**. 10s. should be applied annually in keeping in repair the tomb of her late brother William, at Talygarn, and that any surplus should be paid at Christmas in every year to the minister for the time being of the parish church of Talygarn, to be applied in the purchase of bread for the deserving poor of the said parish.

The other moiety of the annual income is applicable in the parish of St. Fagan's.

In pursuance of an Order of the Board of Charity Commissioners, dated 11th December, 1885, the sum of 83**l**. 6s. 8d. Consolidated 3**l**. per cent. Annuities, sufficient to produce an annual income of 2**l**. 10s. was on the 6th January, 1886 transferred to the account of the Official Trustees of Charitable Funds in trust for the Charity.

The grave referred to is in the churchyard and not in the chapel, so that, under the decisions of the Court of Chancery in Fiske v. The Attorney General and Williams v. The Attorney General, the whole of the income becomes applicable for the purchase of bread, discharged from the obligation of keeping the tomb in repair.

The Rev. William Franklen Evans, head master of Cowbridge School, being the incumbent of the chapelry of Talygarn, receives the dividends, and continues to apply 5s. a year in keeping the tomb in repair; the residue he distributes among the poorest inhabitants of the village of Brynsadler, which lies within this chapelry. Most of the recipients are widows. They receive money doles of two to five shillings.

EVAN EVANS'S CHARITY

Evan Evans, by his Will dated 20th November, 1883, and proved in the principal registry 12th October, 1886, directed as follows:—

> "*I desire to be interred in the vault at Llantrisant in which my father, mother, and brothers are interred, and I direct my executors to purchase the clear sum of* 100l. *Bank* 3l. *per cent Consolidated Annuities and cause the same to be transferred into the names or name of the trustees or trustee for the time being of this my will, or into the name of the rector of the parish church of Llantrisant aforesaid, and that the dividends arising from the said sum of Bank Annuities in every year, shall be paid to or received by the rector and his successors, to the intent that the same shall be applied by him and them in keeping the said vault in repair and proper order, and that if in any year the said dividends shall be more sufficent for the purposes aforesaid, the surplus shall be applied by the said rector and his successors in such manner as he and they may think fit for the benefit of the aforesaid parish. And I direct that the said sum of* 100l. *Consolidated Annuities shall be purchased, and the legacy duty thereon paid, out of my pure personal estate in preference to the other legacies and bequests given and made by this my will, or any codicil thereto.*"

The vault is in the churchyard, and not in the church, so that, under the decisions of the Court of Chancery in Fiske v. Attorney-General, and Williams v. Attorney-General, the whole of the income is discharged from the obligations of keeping the vault in repair, and becomes applicable by the vicar at his discretion.

The executors of his will expended the sum of 33l. 14s. in putting the vault in repair so that the care of it at present entails no expense.

The investment was duly made, and the Consols stand in the name of the Rev. J. Pritchard Hughes, vicar of Llantrisant, who uses the dividends in urgent cases of distress, such as sudden illness or accident.

THOMAS DAVIES'S CHARITIES

By Indenture (dated 29th June, 1811, Thomas Davies of Maesmawr, Pentyrch, granted one clear yearly rent charge or sums of 20l., chargeable upon that tenement of land commonly called Crosstown Farm, situated and lying and being in the parish of Llancarvon, in the County of Glamorgan, and also one clear yearly rent charge or sum of 10l. to be chargeable on all that tenement of land commonly called Broad Close in the said parish, to certain trustees to pay the said rent charge of 10l. unto the preacher or preachers who from time to time should officiate in or for the society of Methodists in the town of Cardiff, and their respective circuits in the said county of Glamorgan, of the religious persuasion of the late John Wesley, and as to the yearly rent charge of 20l. to certain trustees to pay the said sum to the preacher or preachers who should from time to time officiate in or for the society of Methodists in the town of Llantrisant in the said county of Glamorgan, and their respective circuits of the religious persuasion of the said John Wesley.

Broad Close Farm is now in the possession of William Williams, 63 Cardiff Road, Mountain Ash, who regularly pays 10l. to the secretary of the Cardiff Wesley Circuit.

The yearly sum of 20l. issuing from Crosstown Farm, of which Mr. Thomas Jenkins, Gwernydomen, Caerphilly, is the present owner, is applied in augmenting the stipend of the Wesleyan minister at Llantrisant.

Monies from these charities continue to be distributed by the Vicar of Llantrisant.

NON-CONFORMIST PLACES OF WORSHIP

In addition to the Parish Church, several non-conformist places of worship have been established in and near the town, since the second half of the eighteenth century :—

Penuel (Calvinistic Methodist) b. 1775 rebuilt 1826.

Bethel (Welsh Independent) b. 1808, improved 1856.

Zoar (b. 1862 and is now the Church Hall—Independent). Known as Cwrdd uchaf.

(A new church was constructed on the site of Dr. Price's House, Ty'r Clettwr, in 1902).

Wesleyans (b. 1813, improved 1861) present Wesleyan Church at Southgate built 1881. Derelict in 1974.

Trinity (Presbyterian Church of Wales) b. 1876.—This church is now amalgamated with Penuel and the Trinity building and is now a flourishing church with the cause of the Assemblies of God.

Full Gospel Mission Church (1961).

Tabor (Welsh Baptist) b. 1824, rebuilt 1924.

Full Gospel Mission Church, Cross Inn.

Spiritual Church, Penygawsi.

All Hallows Roman Catholic Church, Penygawsi.

6. The Charter of Llantrisant

Borough towns were more strongly fortified, and it is believed that the boundary was sanctified by a religious ceremony, a survival of which is the annual procession for "beating the bounds" still held in many ancient towns. These towns became, wherever suitable, the public stronghold and administrative centre of the district. The chief man in a borough was the reeve, an officer responsible to the King or Lord for the collection of the toll. The borough was usually the centre of church government.

The Normans brought prosperity to the towns and they gained greater freedom by means of charters. A charter is a written contract of privileges granted by the King or barons to communities such as boroughs or gilds. These charters were granted in return for money payments, hence the richer the towns the greater were the privileges which they could obtain. Many charters were granted during time of war for monetary gain. Privileges varied in different boroughs.

From an early period, Llantrisant had been a borough which was first granted a charter in 1346. The present charter is dated 20th Ocober, 1424 and was granted by the Earl of Warwick in the reign of Henry VI. This charter confirms several other Charters granted on previous occasions, the first mentioned being one granted by Hugh de Spenser, Lord of Glamorgan, in 1346, afterwards in 1358, 1397, 1421 and finally 1424. The Charters are dated:—

1346—4th March 20 Edward III.
1358—2nd July 32 Edward III.
1397—18th February 20 Richard II.
1421—24th August 9 Henry V.
1424—20th October 3 Henry VI.

The 1424 Charter was translated into English by order of the Court Leet in 1779, but an entry for 8th April, 1809 states:—

> "*We also Present to hold a Court Leet for settling to subscribe for a copy of the Charter of this Borough on the above mentioned 13th day of May next.*"

This implies that the charter was lost, as were so many records, weights and measures and halberds. The Court officials seem to have had an indifferent attitude to the property and honour of an efficient borough. The charter commenced as follows:—

> "*Richard Earl of Warwick, Lord le Despenser, and of Glamorgan and Morgan, to all the faithful to whom these present letters may be made known, Greeting. We have seen the Charter of Lord Richard de Beauchamp, Earl of Worcester, Lord le Despenser, and of Glamorgan and Morgan, and of Abergavenny, and of Isabella, our wife, which he made to our Burgesses of Llantrisant* . . .

Felin-y-gwynt, Llantrisant

Castle Ruins fom the North

Llantrisant Church from the North West

Interior of Parish Church, circa 1900

Interior of Parish Church before 1873

BELLRINGERS' PHOTOGRAPH

1, The Lord Bishop of Llandaff; 2, Rev. D. H. Simon (Vicar); 3, Rev. C. Rees (Curate); 4, Rev. J. O. Williams, Vicar of Gilfach Goch; 5, John Johns, Vicar's Warden; 6, P. Westcott; 7, W. Huish (Sec.); 8, B. Frances (Treble); 9, F. Bryant (Dpt. Leader); 10, W. Westcott; 11, M. H. Davis, People's Warden; 12, R. John; 13, H. James; 14, L. Davis; 15, J. Evans (Leader); 16, N. Frances; 17, A. E. Powell; 18, R. Wescott.

4th DECEMBER, 1926

Dedication of two New Treble Bells: by the Bishop of Llandaff
Commemorating the completion of the Peal of Eight Bells.

Effigy: Cadwgan Fawr of Miskin

Norman Font

Llantrisant Parish Church: The Nave

The Parish Offices, b. 1873
now the Llantrisant Community Council Offices (1974)

The Town Hall

The Malt House

Toll Cottages, Southgate, b. 1785

Presentation of Mr. Trefor Thomas, Clerk to Town Trust and Major E. T. Davies, Clerk to Parish Council to Her Majesty Queen Elizabeth and the Duke of Edinburgh during the Official Opening of the Mint in December 1968

(Photograph by the Celtic Press)

No. 1988

Llantrisant.

GLAMORGAN.

No.

This is to Certify *that at a Meeting of* **TRUSTEES** *of the Llantrisant Town Trust, held at the Town Hall, Llantrisant,* 15th *day of* August *One Thousand* nine *Hundred and* forty-seven,

TO WIT Major J. R. Ll. Traherne son of Llewellyn Edmund Traherne

was entered on the Town Trust Freemen's Roll of Llantrisant, and paid 18/10 for Fees. 1140

Mathew Thomas
Thomas G Beavan
Hy Alexander
Reg Westcott
[illegible]

Trustees.

Stanley Thomas. Clerk.

A Freeman's Certificate

Beating the Bounds Ceremony, June 1946

Freemen of Llantrisant on Castle Green, June 1946

The Police Station, b. 1876

Fair Day, Llantrisant, Early 1900's

Old Cobbled Streets in Llantrisant

Llantrisant, by J. 'Warwick' Smith, July 3, 1795 *(National Library of Wales)*

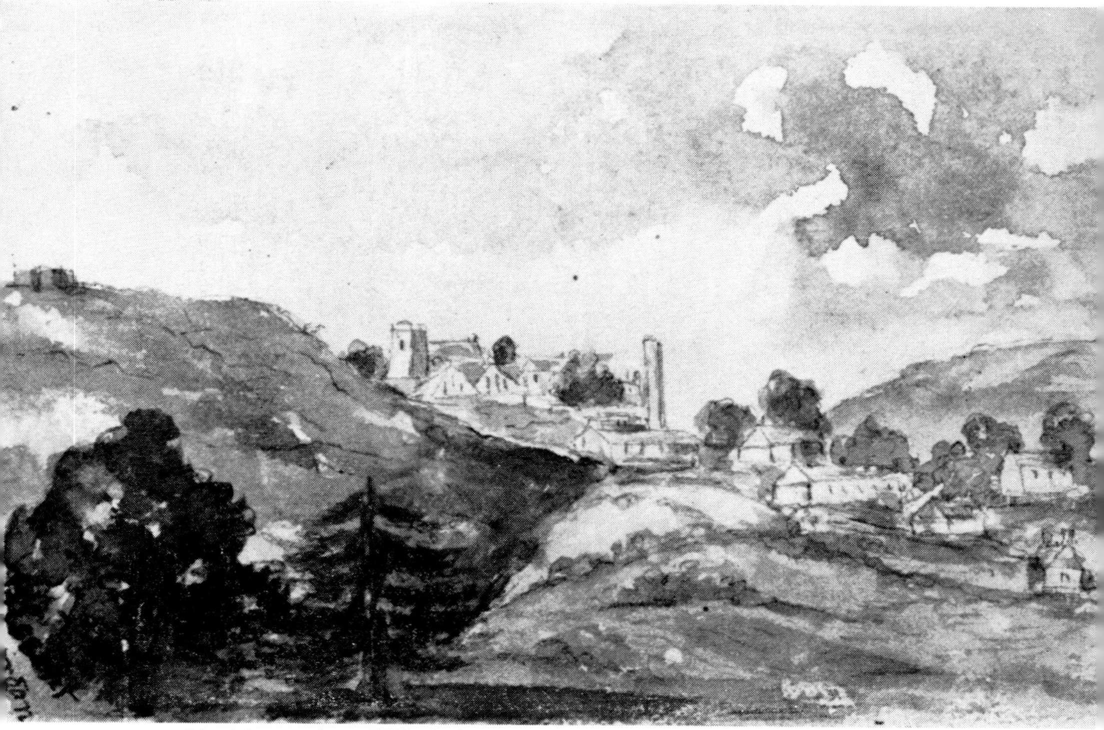

Llantrisant ,circa 1870. Artist unknown *(National Library of Wales)*

Llantrisant, by Joshua Cristall (1767-1847). Not dated

The Common, Llantrisant circa 1910

Llantrisant in 1830

The George Inn (1890's)

Elizabethan House, Llantrisant

"... *Know ye that we have seen the Charter of Lord Hugh le Despencer, our uncle of good memory, Lord of Glamorgan and Morgan, to all bailiffs and their assistants, and to the others of the faithful to whom these present letters may come, Greeting. Know ye, that we of our special grace have granted and by this present Charter do confirm to our well beloved Burgesses of the town of Llantrisant* ...

"... *In testimony whereof we have caused to be affixed to this Charter of our confirmation, the seal of our Chancery of Cardiff in the presence of Sir Oliver St. John, our present Sherriff of Glamorgan, Sir John St. John, Sir John Stradling, Knights; Henry Slake, the Constable of Cardiff Castle, David Mathew, Llewellyn ap Evan Mady, Morgan Llewellyn ap Evan, Esquires and others. Given at Cardiff the 20th of October, in the 3rd year of the reign of King Henry the Sixth, after the conquest.*"

This charter was endorsed in Cardiff, 27th October, 1662, by the Commissioners: Thomas Thomas, John Carne, Henry Bassett.

The Charter granted that Burgesses are free to trade with their merchandize and chattels and free from tolls and they may will their burgages, rents and tenements; Burgesses shall not be constrained to pass beyond their ancient liberties and bounds; Burgesses not to be Receivers of our pence (Lord's taxes) save those arising out of the Bailiwick and that none but burgesses, shall keep a stall, shop or tavern; Burgesses may make taxation amongst themselves, to their own profit and may not be distrained for another's debt; The Lord's Bailiffs cannot distrain or summons; this can only be done by the Constable of the Castle or by the burgesses' bailiff; Merchants may not pass through the town except by the King's highway; No burgess who can find bail may be imprisoned, except for felony; In all inquisitions relating to property, inquisitors to be burgesses; The Lord's constable may make proclamation of Assize of Bread and Ale; The Constable may hold Hundred Courts, monthly, of all pleas and complaints, except the Pleas of the Crown; House-bote and heybote and rights to dead wood in forests and the right to grind corn in the Lord's mills; Right of pannage of hogs, paying to Lord: 1d. for a large hog, ½d. for a pig of a year, for little pigs of lesser age nothing; No foreign bailiff to be coroner, only the Constable of the Castle.

In addition to the above-mentioned privileges, the Burgesses had in their possession and control, long before the first Charter was granted, rights of ownership over certain lands called the "Cymdda" and Graig which comprises the following :—

Acreage of Commons and lands

	a.	*r.*	*p.*
The Graig—	31	1	29
The Common—	246	2	25
Little Common or Cymdda Bach	2	2	36
	284	0	0

The land was divided into Commotes and Cantrefs which was the practice in Wales during this period:—

10 houses	—1 trev (town).
10 trevs	—1 Commote.
10 Commotes	—1 Cantref.
10 Cantrefs	—1 gwlad, cyfoeth arglwydd (lordship)

It is said that the Freeman of Llantrisant acquired the right of grazing their cattle on this common land from Gwrgan a valiant, powerful prince of South Wales. These rights are held at the present time and are jealously guarded.

The Silver Mace dates from 1633 and is older than the Mace in the House of Commons in London.

7. The Court Leet

The Court Leet was made up of a Jury of twelve persons selected by the Sergeant-at-Mace from the Freeman of the town and the usual custom was for one of the Aldermen to be Foreman of the Jury.

The Court met twice a year. During the October meeting, the Jury presented three of the Aldermen for the office of Portreeve, the chief magistrate. Then the Constable of the Castle and Steward of the Court would select the Portreeve for the ensuing year. Three Freemen were also presented from whom the Portreeve selected one to be Sergeant-at-Mace for the ensuing year. At the May meeting, four Burgesses were presented, from whom the Constable of the Castle and Steward selected two to be Overseers of the Market for the ensuing year; they likewise presented further lists of Freemen from which were selected four to be Overseers of the Commons and eight to be Constables. When vacancies occurred among the Aldermen, the Jury of one of the Courts Leet presented a sufficient number of Freemen as Aldermen to fill the vacancies. The Jury, also during this meeting, presented the Burgesses for admission to their Freedom. The Freemen acquired a title to their Freedom in four ways : by birth—every son of an admitted Freeman, whether the father was admitted or not at the time of the birth; by marriage—every person marrying the daughter of an admitted Freeman, whether the father was admitted or not at the time of the birth or marriage of the daughter; by apprenticeship—every person having served an apprenticeship to a Freeman within the Borough; by gift;—every person whom the Jury may think proper to nominate and the Constable of the Castle and the Steward of the Court may think proper.

In practice, the Constable of the Castle and Steward had sometimes declined to swear in persons presented by the Jury for Freedom by gift. The fees on the admission of Freemen were the same in all cases:—

To Borough Chest	—10s. 6d.
To Town Clerk	— 3s. 4d.
To Sergeant-at-Mace	— 2s. 6d.

There were no fees on the admission of any of the other officers. At the present time, an eligible Freeman pays a nominal fee of £8.00 when he is twenty-one years of age. For this, the Freeman gets a parchment with his name and his father's name inscribed on it. This is signed by the Clerk to the Court and by five trustee members who are in office at the time. The present Clerk is Trevor Rees, Esq. The Town Trust is an Associated Body with the Freeman of England. They own the Freehold of the Common land. Duty is no longer paid to the Lord of the Manor.

If the Freeman's father has not made himself a Freeman in his lifetime, then the son loses the right to become one. Also, if the father is a direct descendant, the daughter can make her husband a Freeman, even if she marries more than once. Should the father die, his sons can make themselves Freemen. In this case, the mother cannot make her second husband a Freeman. It is strange, that the daughter has no need to swear herself in to be a Freeman. She inherits the right from her father. The Reverend John Griffith, in his book " Edward II in Glamorgan ", sums up the ceremony by saying, " Freedom of the town is now an archaeological curiosity, now and then presented in a small box to some distinguished person."

It was the duty of the Portreeve to summon and attend the Courts Leet and to receive the fees on the admission of Freemen. The fees and other sums were usually laid out on the repair of the gates and entrance to the Common Lands and Graig, for drainage, general improvements of the Common, and repair of the Town Pump. The Portreeve collected burgage rents within the Borough which were estimated at £9. Instead of these rents the sum of £3 : 1 : 7d. was paid from 1875 to the Lord, the Marquis of Bute. The Town Clerk was appointed by the Lord of the Borough. He received a fee of 3s. 4d. on the admission of every Freeman but had no other fees or emoluments. The Sergeant-at-Mace had to summon the Court Leet by precept from the Portreeve. He acted as Crier of the Court and received a fee of 2s. 6d. on the admission of every Freeman. The Overseers of the Market superintended the market and inspected the weights and measures. At fairs, they were entitled for their own use to a 2d. toll from all non-freemen bringing their wares for sale. The Overseers of the Commons superintended the Commons and prevented the trespassing of strange cattle. They received no emolument but that they might receive from the owners of impounded cattle. The Freemen were to attend the meetings of the Court Leet. They had the right of voting for Membership of Parliament so far as it was left to them by the various Reform Acts. They also had the right of Common use in the Common Land, known as Cymdda and Graig about 284 acres, and other waste lands within the Borough.

The Portreeve, on accepting office made the following declaration :—

" *Glamorganshire*
Borough of Llantrisant.

I, ——————, do solemnly and sincerely in the presence of God, profess, testify and declare upon the true faith of a Christian That I will never exercise any power, authority or influence which I may possess, by virtue of the office of Portreeve of the Borough of Llantrisant, to injure or weaken the Protestant Church, as it is by law established in England, or to disturb the said Church, or the Bishops and Clergy of the said Church in the possession of any rights or privileges to which such Church, or the said Bishops and Clergy, are, or may be by law entitled."

When the Jury took office, the members made a declaration as follows:

The Foreman's oath :

" *You, as Foreman of this Jury, shall enquire and true presentment make of all such things as shall be given you in charge. The King's (or Queen's) council, your own, and your fellows, you shall well and truly keep Secret; you shall present nothing out of malice or hatred nor conceal anything out of love, fear, favour, affection or hope of reward; but in all things you shall well and truly present as the same shall come to your knowledge. So help you God."*

The Freeman's oath :

"*You shall swear to be true to our Sovereign, (Queen Victoria) and the Lords of this Town and Borough; you shall be obedient to the Portreeve of the said Borough, for the time being, and obey his precepts and commands; you shall be civil and obedient to the Aldermen of the same, and also you shall as much as in your power lies, contribute and do every act and thing for the good government and safety of the Borough, and the inhabitants thereof. So help you God etc. . . .*".

Whenever the Court Leet met the following proclamation was made:—

"*Oyez Oyez Oyez. All manner of persons that owe suit and service to this Court Leet, and view of Frank Pledge, of our Sovereign (Lord the King or Lady the Queen), with the Court Baron of the most noble John, Marquis of Bute, Lord of the said Borough, draw near and give your attendance, and answer to your names at the first call, and save your amerciaments God save the King (or Queen), the Lord of the said Borough, the Constable of the Castle, and the Portreeve of the said Borough.*"

The Court closed with :—

"*Oyez Oyez Oyez. All manner of persons, that have appeared this day at this Court Leet, and Court Baron may from hence depart, giving their attendance again on fresh summons. God save the King (or Queen) etc. . . .*".

Presentments at the Court Leet

At the Courts Leet, the custom existed of presenting pieces of waste land within the borough, and subject to the approval of the Lord of the Borough, on payment of small sums varying from sixpence upwards for the pieces of waste land. Some of the original presentments are preserved, among other records, at the County Record Office, Cardiff and in the National Library, Aberystwyth. Many records are lost. The oldest document is dated 1743 and is a list of Freemen submitted in that year at one of the meetings of the Court Leet.

From the records, it can be seen that a variety of subjects was presented and that the officials of the Court were, on several occasions, indifferent to the administration of the borough and to the maintaining of property such as records, halberts, weights and measures etc. These records were lost and found and lost again several times. The following extracts from the records will show this to be the case during the years 1785-1851 :

4th June, 1785:

" We do also present that our Town Prison is filled up with lime and other materials, therefore, we desire that the said Prison be immediately cleaned out and likewise kept clean for the reception of offenders."

30th Sept., 1785:

" also setting forth the **many records of this Court Leet have been lost."**

3rd June, 1786:

" all owner of pigs within this Borough ought to put rings in their noses, for they do make great damage to the Common of this Borough."

4th October, 1794:

" We also present that it is expedient and necessary to walk the limits of this Corporation and do fix on Old Michaelmas Day next for that purpose."

The day for " Beating the Bounds " was kept with great hilarity. It was eagerly anticipated for enjoyment, especially by the young people and the most devoted of the Freemen who wished to maintain the old customs. Once every seven years, about the months of August or September, the Portreeve, Aldermen, Freemen and Officials, met at the Town Hall, where a procession was formed and proceeded to " beat the bounds ". The procession continued along the boundary to various points of note, where the whole company were regaled with refreshments. To commemorate the event, money, fruit and other articles were thrown into the river or old pond, when some of the company usually received a ducking. A still further means of impressing the minds of the children, was for one or two of them to be bumped or whipped on some of the boundary stones. After the perambulation of the boundary, the company returned to the Town Hall.

1st June, 1799:

A complaint was presented that certain persons " have turned scabbed and mangy horses on the Common and being required by them to take them off, have refused so to do. They are therefore fined each for that offence ".

16th May, 1801:

" We present John Hopkins for sinking a draw well on the King's Highway leading from the Borough of Caerphilly, being a public nuisance. Unless removed before 1st July next, to be fined 40s. less 1d."

14th May, 1808:

" We present there should be five new gates made immediately on the Graig and Common."

8th April, 1809:

" We also present to hold a Court Leet for settling to subscribe for a Copy of the Charter of this Borough on the above mentioned 13th day of May next."

13th August, 1814 :

" We also present for the Corporation two new halberds to be paid for by the Lord of the Borough similar to the newest of those now in possession ".

13th November, 1819 :

" Thomas Morgan, Cordwainer, presents that the Overseers of the Common do not do their duty, because cattle belonging to unprivileged persons, are daily grazing on the Common ".

4th May, 1822 :

" The Jurors also present that it would be very desirable that a Pound should be erected on the Common for the purpose of impounding such cattle as trespass thereon, and they recommend that the Lord of the Borough be requested by the Court to erect a Manor Pound on the said Common."

The Common Pound was situated in the castle grounds. This institution existed for centuries and has survived to the present time. The Pound is enclosed by a wall 8 ft. to 9 ft. high, and unlike many others within the boundary of the Corporation, is maintained by the Lord of the Manor, who appoints the pound keeper. In this enclosure, cattle and other animals found straying were retained until redeemed by their owners. The Keeper was obliged to receive everything committed to his custody and not answerable if the animal committed was illegally impounded. When animals were impounded, the impounder had to feed them. The cost of such foods were to be paid by the owner of the animals before they were removed.

19th October, 1822 :

"And the Jurors on their oath aforesaid further present that certain inhabitants, householders residing within this Borough do admit and harbour and lodge certain idle vagabonds and other disorderly persons to the great danger and terror of the town and neighbourhood and that David Thomas, inn-keeper of the Five's Court public house in this town, and Margaret John, spinster of the said Town, are amongst such persons harbouring and lodging such idle vagabonds and disorderly persons, and thereby create a nuisance and that they respectively ought to be fined for the same."

30th September, 1826 :

" The Jury present that the town pump is out of repair and the well required deepening. They recommended that the Portreeve takes measure for effectively repairing, amending and deepening the same. Present boundaries to be perambulated at the first convenient opportunity."

17th November, 1872 :

" The Jurors present that there is a Rent due to the Corporation for the North Turnpike gatehouse, which is considerably in arrears, and that the Portreeve is requested to make a demand for the same."

6th October, 1837 :

"The Jurors request that all Constables having halberts (swords) in their possession are requested to bring in their halberts to Mr. Wm. John, Town Clerk."

7th May, 1847 :

"The Jurors present that the halberts belonging to the Corporation should be sought after and that the Constables of the Court should use their best endeavours to recover them. The weights and measures having been found, they present that the Portreeve should furnish proper scales for the use of the Corporation."

This slackness was later to become one of the main causes for the dissolution of the Borough and Corporation.

27th May, 1851 :

"Present that the Pump on the Bull Ring should be repaired from the funds of the Corporation."

The Bull Ring is a space of ground in the town once used for bull-baiting; the old ring and loop were removed to a spot on the Common. It was presented in 1770 that :—

"The Jury present that the Corporation is deficient of a Head rope for bull-baiting." In 1827, "that bull-baiting was disallowed". The Town Hall or Guild Hall was only presented a few times, in 1734 and 1744 for repair, in 1749 for being "in ruin", in 1756 for repair; in 1773 it was presented that a new Guild Hall and corn market be erected by the Lord of the Manor. The Guild Hall was built in 1773 under the patronage of Lady Windsor, the Lady of the Borough and Manor at that time. The lower portion was formerly the corn market but in 1896 it was converted into a library and reading room.

When in 1835, Commissioners on the Municipal Corporations visited the town to make their first report they were displeased with the state of the town and its inhabitants in general. The result was that the Corporation was dissolved in 1883.

The Lord of the Manor still held his Court Leet for his manors at the Town Hall, Llantrisant after the dissolution. A jury was impanelled, constables appointed and presentments made. The Court was held annually. Notices for a Court in 1897 are as follows :—

Courts Leet

Glamorgan

"Notice is Hereby Given that the Courts Leet of our Sovereign Lady the Queen and General Courts Baron of the Most Honourable John Patrick Crichton-Stuart Marquess of Bute and Earl of Dumfries Baron Cardiff of Cardiff Castle K.T., Lord of the several Manors hereinafter named will be holden at the several places and on the several Days following that is to say :—

For the Manors of Miskin cum Membris Pentirch and Clun at the Town Hall Llantrisant on Friday the 15th October next at One o'clock in the afternoon.
When and where all persons who owe Suit and Service to the several Courts are required to attend and pay their respective quit and Chief Rents, Fines and other payments due to the Lord of the several Manors.

William Thomas Lewis
John Stuart Corbett
Stewards."

Bute Estate Office,
Cardiff, Sept. 1st 1897.

8. The Parish Vestry of Llantrisant

Today, local government is as important as the central government, because it deals with our immediate problems. In Norman times, local government was in the hands of the lord of the manor. As time passed, changes were inevitable. Manors changed hands and gradually the Manorial System declined. By the time of the Tudors, the important division in local government was the parish. The manor was now comparatively unimportant, most matters being conducted from the church.

Behind the church building was the vestry in which the Vicar, or incumbent, dressed for service. This room was found to be very convenient as a meeting place for the leading land-owners of the parish and it became the practice for these to hold meetings in the vestry, usually under the chairmanship of the incumbent, to discuss local affairs. The Vestry became very powerful and its duties covered a wide field. The Common Lands were administered, roads kept in reasonable order and the church maintained. Much of the work was in the hands of parish officers. It was not until the end of the nineteenth century when people were getting more democratic ideas, that the parish oligarchy was destroyed and local boards, elected by the rate-payers, established. Today the Vestry is only concerned with church affairs in the Parish.

The Parish Officers were : the Church Wardens, the Constable, the Surveyor of the Highways (1555) and the Overseers of the Poor (1597). The system of appointed officers varied in each locality. In many parishes they were elected by the " House-Row " system whereby the office passed indiscriminately from one householder to the next. In other parishes elections were held, but only the Vestry could elect officers and often these had to be approved by the Justices of the Peace. The holding of these offices was not relished, because they were mostly unpaid and the holder was put to considerable hardship before his term of office expired. Some had to be compelled to take office by the Justices of the Peace.

A selection of quotations from the vestry books gives a picture of life in the town. Charity was the principal feature of the parish system and its distributors were two overseers, with a yearly salary, appointed and paid by the parish vestry. Their official title was " Overseers of the Poor ". In nearly all cases the needs of the poor were met by what was then generous treatment. Like most privileges, parish relief was notoriously abused. Under the system, a man could receive either money or equipment with which to earn a living. On 23rd August, 1782, it was ordered that " a spinning wheel be given to Cecil Evan ".

Those workers who were underpaid were helped by the parish. Unscrupulous employers deliberately underpaid their employees, thus forcing the parish to bear the burden. Children maintained by the parish were quickly apprenticed. An order to apprentice such children was made on 23rd August, 1782, noting " that the Overseers of the Poor " do not neglect their duty in this respect. A woman who had left her home town to live with her husband would be stranded on his death, for it was held in law that she could only reside " on the parish " in her home town. On 27th December, 1872, an order " for removing Jane, the widow of Thomas Morgan Evan, Carpenter, and their children is approved by us, to the parish of Llanharan, and if the parishioners of Llanharan shall appeal against the said order, we will indemnify the Overseers of the Poor of our said parish of Llantrisant ". Responsibility was passed from one authority to another.

Even in 1783 there was a free health service for the poor. In that year, a Mr. Watkin Evans was the " surgeon and apothecary " for the parish and charged to "attend the poor and supply them with plaster, medicines, etc., and also foreigners for whom our Overseer shall apply ". For this service, he was paid a quarterly salary of one guinea. Doctors had to make life as tolerable as possible for people suffering from mental illness. There is an entry in the vestry book for 8th December, 1796 which states: " David Harry was allowed 3s. 6d. weekly for ' maintaining and taking care of Mary David being lunatic ' ".

Perhaps the most historic meeting of the vestry was called on 5th December, 1783, " to consult in regard of establishing a workhouse for the Poor of Llantrisant ". A workhouse was to be built at Llantrisant and contracts given to John Popkins, Esq., of Talygarn. Margaret Jenkin, a widow, was engaged as a superintendent " to see the poor fed, put to work and to weigh and measure every article used in the said house ". She had to record the sale of anything for which she was paid " £12 a year, fire, meat, candles and one room for her use, her wages to be paid weekly ". A male superintendent, Thomas Jenkin, was paid an annual salary of £18. A Treasurer, Mr. Evan Jones, a shopkeeper, received £5 a year. If the supervisors " be minded to use any tea or coffee or sugar, this is to be at their own expense ".

On 4th February, 1784, another meeting was called to discuss the establishment of a workhouse. John Popkins Esq., was ordered to apply to Lord Cardiff, Lord of the Manor, and to the burgesses of the town for " land containing one or more acres of the Graig Common, on which to erect the work-house with all necessary conveniences". At the meeting on 28th April, 1784, it was ordered that the workhouse be made ready for the reception of the poor by Monday, 10th May, 1784. On 5th May, 1784, it was unanimously resolved " that the poor be humanely and properly treated, and that Watkin Evans do constantly and daily attend the poor in the workhouse ". In an article published in the " Western Mail " in October 1937, " The First Workhouse in Glamorgan ", the opening, procedure, rules and diet in the workhouse are recorded. The article states that " Prior to 1784, the aged, feeble or weak-minded, all of whom came under the general title of paupers, were either left in insanitary cottages in the village, usually called poor-houses, or were farmed out to be fed and cared for by a neighbour, who was paid a small weekly sum ". The only thing done well by the parish council was the burial of dependants. The workhouse was established " to the end of rendering more humane treatment of the poor and as ease of the load of taxes on the parishes and being encouraged by an Act of Parliament, the said house at Llantrisant has been established on a certain plan ". The plan was that a fixed rate be charged and that the rates be paid to an appointed treasurer and that the trustees " shall meet every Friday at the Governor's house to peruse the accounts and expenditure ".

THE DIET

Tuesday, 11th May :	*Breakfast*: milk porridge *Dinner*: beef and roots *Supper*: broth
Wednesday, 12th May :	*Breakfast*: milk porridge *Dinner*: flummery and milk *Supper*: milk porridge
Thursday, 13th May :	*Breakfast*: milk porridge *Dinner*: beef or mutton and roots *Supper*: broth
Friday, 14th May :	*Breakfast*: broth *Dinner*: flummery and milk *Supper*: milk porridge
Saturday, 15th May :	*Breakfast*: milk porridge *Dinner*: bread and butter and roots *Supper*: broth
Sunday, 16th May :	*Breakfast*: milk porridge *Dinner*: beef and roots *Supper*: broth
Monday, 17th May :	*Breakfast*: broth *Dinner*: bread and cheese and beer *Supper*: milk porridge

In the weekly bill of fare, milk was the most prominent in the diet. There was a rule about the diet table. The Governor was allowed to vary the diet, if the majority so desired, to apples and rice, rice and milk, apple dumplings, apple pudding or rice pudding.

The rules of the institution were many, and several appear to be odd to us today. The following selection will bear this out :—

(1) *" The upper garment of the poor to be all of the same colour and badged with the letters L. P. in red."*

(2) *" The poor to be washed clean on entering the house."*

(3) *" No poor shall be allowed to go out of the doors except by leave of the governor."*

(4) *" If any leave work and plead ailment they are to be examined by the doctor, if this prove false to be punished by the loss of the next meat, but if they still refuse to work they are to be sent to the " House of Correction."*

Hours of work were long

(5) *"All poor who are able shall work from six in the morning till seven in the evening from Lady Day (9th April) to Michaelmas (29th Sept.) and from seven till six from Michaelmas to Lady Day."*

(6) *"The rooms of the said house be kept clean and swept or washed three times a week. The windows frequently left wide open and that wormwood be used to fumigate the rooms, to wash the linen and also to be in the beds."*
Wool—*Gave wool to workers to encourage industry the sum of 1d. per pound of wool made into yarn was given to each worker and "the poor may expend the money so earned in any way and by any means they think proper."*

(7) *"At the close of the day's work the Bible is to be read aloud to the poor for half-an-hour, and on Sundays, such as are able, must go to the church or else to some other place of public worship."*

(8) *"No persons may smoke in the bedrooms or upstairs."*

An inaugural meeting of the trustees was held in the Governor's Room on 17th May, 1784. An entry in the records for 22nd April, 1785 states:—

"John Popkin to contract with the Reverend Gervis Powell for an additional building to the workhouse."

Conditions were fairly crowded and so on 23rd December, 1785, it was decided to purchase a farm called "Wern-y-Mole Fawr" for the use of the workhouse. An entry in the vestry book for 25th May, 1796 is in contrast to the above :—

"If any pauper shall at any time make an application to a Justice for relief 'then vestry meeting called' and all the poor of the said parish shall be immediately rented out to the highest bidder." The records give proof of heated debates at the vestry meeting. They are registered by the rapid contradiction of decisions.

4th July, 1796 :
Agreed that "not to let out the poor in the workhouse to any person or persons".

11th July, 1796 :
"Agreed to let out eleven children from the workhouse to Mr. Plummer of Bridgend in this county, a clothier, to work in his factory". But this was withdrawn on 18th July—a counter order was made. Finality was reached by 10th September, 1800, when no one was let out. The Overseers of the Poor were to "take care and provide for them".

Intimacy in the Parish system of government was important in order that the needs of persons be met. An entry for 15th July, 1785 bears this statement :—

"Whereas, Margaret Llewellyn has this day applied for a shirt, handkerchief and apron, and says that on having the same, she

will set out immediately for Cornwall or elsewhere, where she states she has been invited to come by some or others of her acquaintance, we grant the said request."

During this period, when press gangs went around forcibly conscripting men into His Majesty's Navy, intimacy could have been a disadvantage. A record for 7th March, 1783, resolved " that £8 be paid by the Overseers of the Poor towards the redeeming of Thomas John now on Board the Elizabeth, Man of War, one of His Majesty's Ships, a churchwarden was paid £8 to perform this negotiation ". Orders relating to national requirements appeared on occasions :—

"Appoint three men " for raising a certain number of men for the service of His Majesty's Navy ". This record is dated 10th March, 1786. A meeting, relating to this order was called for 31st March, 1786 when the Overseers of the Poor and Churchwardens met at the Cross Keys Hotel.

A meeting in the New Inn on 27th August, 1795 stated " John Hopkins, the former churchwarden and John Jones, former Overseer of the Poor, were allowed £19 : 8 : ½d. and £32 : 1 : 0d. respectively for their trouble and service in recruiting three volunteers to serve in His Majesty's Navy and for paying their bounty ". (Sums for bounty were collected in Llantrisant and the Hamlet of Hafod in Llanwonno and to reimburse parishes for recruiting expenses). " Healthy, able men between 16 yrs. to 45 yrs. of age with not above two children " were sought. Just how willing were those same volunteers is seen by an entry dated 20th Nov., 1796, allowing 14s. to David Thomas, former churchwarden, for his trouble in guarding the volunteers for three days and two nights ! By 1804 there was an order, issued on 15th March from the New Inn, commanding the parish officers to " Find a proper person to serve in the militia.

The eighteenth century, with its collections for the poor, and bounties for servicemen gave ample opportunity for the various persons concerned to embezzle funds. On 3rd October, 1796, it was agreed " not to allow Thomas Hopkins accounts because we are fully convinced that his accounts were wrong and that he did embezzle the parishioners' money collected by him as rates for use of the Poor ".

There is an entry in the " Guinness Book of Records " which mentions one Lewis Hopkins, a dwarf, who, according to the following certificate was born somewhere in the Parish of Llantrisant :—

" *This is to certify that Lewis Hopkin, the bearer thereof, is a man of a very honest character, and had six children. His second son, Hopkin, whom you now see with him, is in the fifteenth year of his age; not exceeding* 2 *ft.* 7 *ins. in height, and about* 12 *or* 13 *lbs. weight, wonderful to the sight of all beholders: the said little man was baptized the 29th January* 1736, *by me, R. Harris, Vicar of Llantrisant, Glamorgan."*

The father of Lewis Hopkin took his son about the country to exhibit him, and the above certificate was given to the father to show the public as a guarantee that no deception was practised upon them.

9. Fairs and Markets in Llantrisant

In Llantrisant, four fairs were held annually on 1st May, 13th May, 1st August and 18th October, and Friday was market day. The fairs and markets were the result of the commercial needs of the inhabitants who met regularly together at a given point. The market was not a popular or tribal right, but the King's prerogative. The privilege was independent of the ordinary municipal franchises. Normally the grant was made by the Crown. Sometimes it was designed to attract settlers; sometimes to provide a new source of revenue, either in the shape of a payment for the privilege or the receipt of tolls or both combined. The right to hold a market was not granted indiscriminately.

The fairs were held in the open square. Adjoining the Town Hall, was the former old market house, forming a square with stalls on each side and the Town Hall with the corn market underneath forming the fourth side. In part of this old market were kept the old town scales and weights and other appliances required by the old corporation. The site, when not in use, could not be used for depositing stores or rubbish and a date was usually fixed so that the land might be prepared by the erection of stalls and booths because all stalls had to be removed when the fair was not being held. The stalls were arranged in rows like streets, each street was given a name according to the particular commodity sold in it. There was a formal opening ceremony which took place on a saint or holy day. Markets were held on any weekday (including Sundays), but Friday was chosen as the market day at Llantrisant.

When a fair or market was held in the town, various officers had to fulfil certain duties. The chief official was the Royal official, the Clerk of the Market or Measures. He regulated business by collecting dues and tolls which belonged to the King. Sometimes the burgesses would be granted assay of weights and measures and other appliances belonging to the market. They helped to fix the prices of goods to be sold. In Llantrisant, the duty of collecting dues and tolls fell to the Constable of the Castle. The police or watchmen were provided by the people themselves. They had to enforce the laws against practices of forestalling, regrating and engrossing; that is, any practice which led to the intervention of a middle man between the producer and the consumer. They were on the look out for dishonest travellers. When found they were fined.

Tolls figured largely on market and fair days and on certain commodities at all times. They were imposed on goods entering the town or exposed for sale at the fair or market. There were transit dues which helped to repair the baronial roads and bridges, entrance dues which paid for the upkeep of the town walls, and sale dues. The toll system divided the inhabitants and natives of the surrounding district into two distinct classes: the penalised and the privileged, who were sometimes burgesses of the town. Foreign merchants who brought goods in the town, had to pay all dues on the first Friday Market and every Friday he stayed; otherwise, his merchandise was forfeited to the use of the commonalty. All merchandise had to be shown to either the Constable of the Castle or the Portreeve before it could be sold or removed. In this way the merchants were protected by the town.

The custom of the Market of Llantrisant relating to butchers is as follows (1789): —

		£	s.	d.
	Pitching			1
Standing	for 1 beef			8
	for 1 pig			6
	for a porker cut and hung up in quarters			2
	for a calf			2
	for a sheep or lamb			2

In 1789, at Cardiff Castle, an agreement was signed by several butchers using the market at Llantrisant and stated: —

> " *Whereas the undermentioned Butchers have promoted the finishing of the said Market Place, and have signed an agreement to make use of the same when finished, I do therefore order that when the said market place is finished, that all subscribing butchers who are Burgesses of Llantrisant be at liberty to pitch their own sheds and make use thereof Gratis in the same manner as they now do in the present Market Place. That all the subscribing butchers do pay no more for pitching and standing, than what they are accustomed to do at present.*"

A record dated 19th April, 1786 comments on the state of Tolls:

> " *Tolls are on the decline for several years and declares that they are amazingly reduced this year that he has not collected his bass rent by many pounds*: —

Cattle Tolls

> " *Bute principally, almost all dealers in cattle, now of late, have (or pretend to have) tickets or licences from some places exempting them from paying Tolls in any place in the Kingdom except their own. Duchy (of Lancaster)—those exemptions are brought from Warwickshire, Staffordshire, Gloucestershire, Kidwelly, Talyfan etc., which has reduced this Toll from its old standing rent of four pounds to nothing.*"

A proviso existed that merchants must travel by highways or borough towns "that the Lord lose not his toll". The following table of toll rates will give an idea what was paid by people entering the borough: —

Horse or Mare	4d.
Ox or Cow	2d.
Sheep	½d.

The Cremation of Dr. William Price at Llantrisant, 1893

(*National Library of Wales*)

Crowds at the Cremation of Dr. William Price in January 1893
Showing his children, Nicholas and Penelopen in centre

Miss Penelopen Price, Unveiling Plaque to Memory of Her Father, Dr. William Price, at Zoar Chapel, September, 1947

Talbot Road—1958

Tonysguboriau (Talbot Green) 1958

CONFIRMATION DAY
Bishop Joshua Pritchard Hughes and Curates of Llantrisant

ORPHEUS GLEE SOCIETY, LLANTRISANT, 1920

S. Hayward   J. Lukey   J. I. Williams   J. Barkle   W. Griffiths

L. Evans   J. Venables (*Accompanist*)   E. Llewellyn   J. Lamerton   H. H. Richards   H. Warburton   W. Morgan

T. Dyer   G. Williams   D. Lukey   B. Gregory Evans, R.C.M. (*Conductor*)   F. Wareham (*Organising Sec.*)   W. Davies   I. Pickford

The Llantrisant Male Voice Choir at the Opening of the Royal Mint in 1968
with their Conductor Luther Jones (*Photograph by Celtic Press*)

Two views of Hensol Castle, Pontyclun

Dr. William Price in Druidic Costume

(*National Library of Wales*)

Dr. William Price in 1861
(*National Library of Wales*)

QUEEN VICTORIA'S JUBILEE, 1897

Group of Old Inhabitants on Castle Green after being entertained to tea

LLANTRISANT WAXWORKS 1898

Britannia
Miss M. A. John

Ireland Miss G. Davies		*Wales* Miss K. Edwards	*England* Miss K. Lewis		*Scotland* Miss M. Lewis
Indian Wife Miss L. Hole	*Indian Chief* J. Barkle	*Funny Tom* B. Davies	*P.C.* J. P. John	*Weary Will* T. John	*Italy* Miss M. Morgan
Switzerland Miss G. Evans	*Tommy Atkins* Mr. Whitehead	*Attendant* W. Frances	*Coster Wife* Miss E. Lear	*Conductor* Mr. D. Lukey	*Grace Darling* Miss K. Davies
Violinist J. Stephens	*Vanity* Miss Trailer	*Nurse* Mrs. King		*Tired Tom* D. E. Owen	*Mrs. Flanagan* Miss L. Cook
Empress of Japan Mrs. Morris	*Emperor* Mr. L. Davies	*Japanese Maiden* Miss M. Frances		*Coster* T. Davies	*Violinist* W. H. Owen

Llantrisant Town Crier, Thomas David (Gweydd-Weaver) 1847-1906

Miskin Manor

Interior, St. David's Church, Miskin

The Modern Miskin Village

Miskin Village in 1910

Building St. Paul's Church, Pontyclun, 1894

John Studt's Show which travelled the District in the 1890's and Early Years of this Century

1912: The Jolly Boys Outing at Pontyclun driven by Adrian Trivett Esq., Pontypridd
The Leyland vehicle in the picture was the first bus in South Wales

Commercial Street, Llantrisant

The Bull Ring in the 1890's

Lanelay Hall 1966

High Street, Llantrisant

Goats	—
Pigs	½d.
Geese	—
Raw Hide	(½d.—1d.)
Horseload of Corn	½d.
Horseload of flour / Bale of Wool	4d.
Every entire cloth	½d.
Butter Cheese (Horseload)	½d.
Honey (Horseload)	½d.

Horse-Fairs are also mentioned in the records of the Court Leet. They were duly appointed to check dealings in stolen horses and these fairs had to be held separately from all other fairs. This order was contained in an act passed in 1555. A later act (1589) required a record to be kept of all horses sold at the fairs. A record dated 31st October, 1795 states:

> "*We also do order the Horse Fair to be held on Heol-y-Sarn in this Borough in future.*"

In 1844 (26th April) it was presented that:—

> "*The Horse Fair should be held alternately in Swan Street, commencing* 13*th May,* 1844."

The alternative place was probably where the Market House was situated. The police station stands there today.

Corn Tolls

"The establishing of our workhouse (which was thought would be of great advantage to our market) has reduced the purchasing power of corn there materially—the poor therein having always used to buy their pecks etc., or corn there; whereas there has not been a grain of corn or a pound of meat bought in our market for their supply this last twelve months, all being purchased in private jobs among the rules thereof (100 Bushels above 250 Winchesters of corn are said to be in the Workhouse now)."

Toll-paying seemed to have differed at various times and in order to find out what tolls had been paid at Llantrisant, an examination of witnesses concerning Tolls paid at Llantrisant was carried out on 6th October, 1817. The findings were as follows:—

1. Richard John (76): Heard of toll paid 2 or 3 years ago.
2. James Morgan (68): Heard that a Mr. Bassett paid toll at the Malt House.
3. Ann Miles (70): She knew all grain was subject to toll of measure or even exchanges into different bags within the limits of the borough. She never heard it refused to be paid until of late.

4. Thomas Rimboll	:	Knew that there was toll for all grain and had often paid it himself. He heard that barley converted into Malt was exempted from toll. He lived 21 years in Llantrisant.

Witnesses agreed that all grain in the Borough paid toll and that "All Freemen of the Borough, if they take in their own measure, are exempt from toll, and in the event of using the Market measure, are only liable to pay the one half ".

Road Tolls

In 1745 roads were exactly what they had been in the Middle Ages. The only guiding principle was that the Highway provide " convenient passage " for the " King's subjects ". The entire responsibility for the maintenance of highways rested with the parish. By 1785 the last Post Boys carried mail on the main routes. In 1784 the Post Office had its own Mail Coaches. They were exempt from payment of tolls as stated in the Turnpike Act. Rectors, vicars and curates were also exempt.

Turnpikes

Toll gates were let to Collectors, either annually or for three years and were put up for auction. The defects of the Turnpike system became apparent and in 1845 an Act of Parliament vested authority of Turnpike Trusts in the County Roads Board which met on 12th February, 1845. Glamorgan was divided into a Western, Eastern and Northern District. Llantrisant was in the Northern District.

Now that there is under construction a new trunk road for South Wales which passes near Miskin and Talygarn near Llantrisant, recalls another important cross country route known today as Llantwit Main. The road connects Pontypridd with the Llantrisant-Cardiff main road via Cross Inn and Mwyndy. The route was constructed in 1829 by Mr. William Crawshay who had his house at Hensol Castle and Mr. Richard Hill who was interested in the property at Treforest. Roads were poor here and this road would be a convenient route from Pontypridd to his house at Hensol. It would cut off the steep descent from Llantrisant to Newbridge (Pontypridd). The road would ultimately have been a beneficial one being a convenient way of delivering supplies to the new market at Pontypridd from the Vale of Glamorgan. The route is eight miles long.

A member of the parish was expected to serve as surveyor without payment and parishioners themselves provided the labour, horses, carts and tools.

Some laxity either in presenting accounts or paying them is evident in most trusts, Cardiff Trust paid its surveyor as recorded in 1783:—

> " *Ordered that the sum of twenty pounds be paid to John Price, Esq., Surveyor of the Cross Vane Road for the repairs of the said road.*

The accounts of John Price Esq., Surveyor of the Cross Vane Road were examined and allowed of when there appeared a balance of Twenty five Pounds, nineteen shillings and 11½d. due to the Accountant which is ordered to be paid by the Treasurer."

In 1832:—

"*Complaints having been made by the surveyor that he has not been able to obtain payment of the differences orders of the 10th August last by the Treasurer ordered that the Treasurer do forthwith pay the surveyor the above sums."*

In 1837:—

"*It is ordered that the auditing of the surveyor's accounts with the Trust be postponed until the meeting of the Commissioners this day fortnight when he is desired to attend with same for that purpose and if not more than three Commissioners should attend on that day week they are requested to examine the said surveyor's accounts and report on same.*

The Trustees having taken the same into consideration it is resolved that they find it expedient thereafter to take into their own hands the management of the repairing of the Turnpike Roads."

A constant duty of the Surveyor's in this Trust was that of widening of the narrow country lanes. In 1832 it was "Ordered that the Treasurer do pay the surveyor ten pounds towards the widening of the road near Pendoylan Church and a further sum of ten pounds to be paid out from Crofta to Miskin Bridge in widening the road near Crofta . . ." and the enforcing of the cleansing of ditches, hazards and watercourses, at one time the threat being made that until such was seen to no more money would be spent on the roads. On 20th December 1833:—

"*. . . the surveyor of this Trust having been ordered to give notice to have the hazards and drains opened and the hedges properly plashed and cut which has not yet been done . . . ordered the surveyor is not to lay any more money except in opening underground drains and culverts until the hazards are properly opened."*

For anything more than routine repairs, the surveyor of the Merthyr District, Mr. William Rowlands was called in to give his advice on 13th September 1833 "Ordered that an application be made to W. Rowlands, surveyor, for the probable expense of making a survey and estimate of the new line of road from Llantrisant to Newbridge formerly intended." Modern travellers through Llantrisant know of Southgate Turnpike. A reference was made to it in 1836:—

"*It is hereby ordered that the clerk will forthwith write to Mr. Wm. Rowlands, surveyor Merthyr, to survey and make the best new line of road that can be adopted from the South Turnpike Gate across the New Mill Road to and towards a place called Corner y Park on the foresaid Turnpike Road leading to Cardiff."*

Meetings were advertised in the press. This is one for a meeting on 5th February 1836:—

LLANTRISSENT TURNPIKE TRUST

Notice is hereby given that the Trustees of the said Turnpike Trust will meet at the Cross Keys Inn in the town of Llantrissent on Friday, the 5th day of February next at twelve o'clock at noon, for the purpose of Electing Trustees or Commissioners in the room of such Trustees who have died or become disqualified.

Wm. Jacob, Clerk to the said Trustees.

Llantrisant 9th January, 1836

Turnpike roads were set up by Parliament in Acts passed in 1756, 1799 and 1810. These were "disturnpiked" in 1870 and declared main roads under the Highways and Locomotives (Amendment) Act 1878 and eventually placed under the management of the County Councils.

10. Llantrisant in Nineteenth Century

The period 1800-1883 marks the last phase in the history of Llantrisant as a borough. The other borough, Cowbridge, remains one to this day but because of inefficiency in administration and the appearance of the town, Her Majesty's Commissioners did not see fit to retain the status of borough of the town.

During this period cultural life was flourishing in the town. Several Eisteddfodau were held in public houses during this period and it was not unusual to find people of note and high standing presiding at these meetings. The Eisteddfodau were organised by the Cymreigyddion Society, which was formed at the Swan Inn in the year 1771 and the society was patronised by several gentlemen from the district. The object of the society was to promote Welsh literature, poetry and music. The society was at the height of its power and success during the period 1839-1845. In 1865, a very successful Eisteddfod was held in the old market place, the object being to raise funds to establish a Reading Room and Library at Llantrisant. The sum of £30 was handed over to the Committee, who purchased a small library of books, and through the Marquis of Bute, a room had been placed free of charge to the patrons of the Reading Room.

About the year 1868, a great commotion was caused among the body of freemen by the action of the Lord of the Manor, through his Trustee, having consented and given permission to T. Powell, Esq., to search for coal under the Common Lands. The freemen, having the rights of the Common, were led to believe that they had a perfect right to the minerals underlying the Common. Operations were begun to mine the coal, and the freemen rose up in arms against the operators. They stated that their rights were being infringed and that they should be compensated for damages caused to their surface rights in searching for minerals. The question was often raised, how the Lord of the Manor came possessed of the Minerals.

Previous to the purchase of the Manorial Rights by Sir William Herbert in the year 1551, from Edward VI, the various manorial rights, privileges and customs, had reverted to the Crown. When Sir William Herbert (Lord Bute's predecessor in title) had the grant and particulars of the said Manors, there is no doubt that all manorial rights, including the rights to the minerals, was conveyed in that grant, and have been held down to the present day (1898). There does not appear to be any reservation of mineral rights mentioned in the said grant, according to recent translations.

Mr. G. T. Clark in his "Land of Morgan" mentions a "grant to Sir William Herbert was divested Jura Regalia and other obsolete rights and privileges. The manorial rights remained, and with them the rights to the minerals under the Common Lands". (Grant of several manors in South Wales to Sir William Herbert in 1550 by Edward VI.) Mining operations continued and the workings were still standing until quite recently.

Changes were taking place. Industry was coming to Llantrisant but the importance of the town was diminishing in favour of Pontypridd. Llantrisant became less imposing as a central authority. Gradually, after the opening of the Glamorgan Canal in 1795 and the Taff Vale Railway in 1841, Rhondda coal was brought down to the canal and afterwards, some of it was loaded into wagons at Hafod. Pontypridd gradually emerged into a town and a commercial centre. The Petty Sessions Court was held in Llantrisant until November 1956 when it was transferred to Talbot Green. It does not appear that the Portreeve, as chief magistrate, exercised any magisterial duties in the town during the nineteenth century. All magisterial functions are now exercised by the County Magistrates for the Petty Sessional Division of Miskin Lower.

Every Freeman or Burgess had a parliamentary vote and for this reason, the freedom of the borough was valuable. In Llantrisant, the Borough was only about one fifth of the Parish. The total population of the Parish in 1831 was 2,789 and the number of Borough electors registered under the Act of 1832 was 211. Before the Reform Act of 1832, the following Boroughs voted jointly to send one member to Parliament. This was the Cardiff and Contributory Boroughs Constituency:—

Cardiff	*Llantrisant*	*Aberavon*	*Swansea*
Cowbridge	*Kenfig*	*Neath*	*Loughor.*

In the election of 1820, the borough of Llantrisant registered 120 votes for a member. After 1832, Cardiff, Cowbridge and Llantrisant jointly returned one member, until the reform of 1918 when Llantrisant was included in the Pontypridd Constituency and has been represented by the following Members of Parliament:—

Arthur Lewis, Esq., M.P.

Maerdy Jones, Esq., M.P., until 1930, d. 1970.

D. L. Davies, Esq., M.P., 1930—1938

Arthur Pearson, Esq., M.P. 1938—1970

Brynmor John, Esq., M.P. 1970—

Winston Griffiths, Esq., M.P., European Parliament, 1979

About two hundred and fifty years ago there were very few schools in Wales. Among the first were those sponsored by the Society for the Promotion of Christian Knowledge. One of the leading Welsh supporters was Sir John Phillipps of Picton Castle. They were known as Charity Schools and such a school was established at Llantrisant in the eighteenth century. In 1740, Vicar Harris of Llantrisant applied to Griffith Jones for a school.

This school was replaced by one set up at the Town Hall and Corn Market and patronised by Lord Bute who contributed funds for their maintenance.

In 1865 Canon Powell Jones, B.D. became the Vicar of Llantrisant.

It was during his incumbency that National Schools were set up in the parish:—*Llantrisant National School* 1867, *extended* 1897.
Pontyclun National School 1878.

The schools at Llantrisant were built on part of West Caerlan, the property of the Earl of Talbot and Shrewsbury, who presented the land for the use of the school. The buildings, which cost over £2,000, were used as Llantrisant Primary School until 1976. They are now used by Llantrisant Welsh School with Mr. John Pugh as headteacher. A new school opened on Monday, 2nd September, 1974 was built in open plan style overlooking Llantrisant Common. This school has been named Coed yr Esgob Primary School with Mr. Clive Rickard as headteacher. Another new school was opened at Penygawsi in January 1976 with Mr. John Humphreys as the first headteacher who retired in 1980. The present headmistress is Mrs. Esme Davies.

Canon J. Powell Jones was born on 4th April, 1833 at Llysnony, Gorseinon, Swansea. He received his early education at Loughor National School and then at Bowen's Academy, Swansea where he distinguished himself as the best scholar. At 17 years of age he entered St. David's College, Lampeter, and there was appointed assistant tutor, before he was 22 years of age. He was much influenced by Dr. Ollivant. In 1846, Canon Jones became curate of Loughor Church, where he had been brought up. He was regarded as one of the rising hopes of the Church in Wales. He was in manner refined, elegant and engaging; in appearance dignified, and commanding. He spoke at all times with meekness and moderation but with great authority. His theology was the result of hard and conscientious thinking. Long before dawn each day he would be in his study reading the word of God in the two original languages. He possessed the singular gift of imparting knowledge to others. He was Vicar of Llantrisant (1865-1883), and passed away at the Vicarage, Llantrisant on Friday, 21st December, 1883 and was buried at Llangyfelach. In his death the church lost one of its ablest defenders and education one of its truest friends. He has earned himself a niche in the "temple of theological fame" by the admirable manner in which he defended the teachings of the Church.

Llantrisant seemed to be a progressive parish in looking after people. Its funds were supplemented by charitable requests. On 1st January, 1806, it is recorded "that the milk cow which the late Mrs. Catherine Powell, a widow, did leave, is now old—and the poor of the Hamlet of Trane in this Parish are deprived from the use and benefit of the said cow". The document also relates that she had given to seven poor people near her dwelling house, the use and benefit of one milk cow for ever, together with 2s. 6d. to each of them every Candlemas Day for ever. There were no hard and fast rules for receiving benefit. The problems of the poor depended on the good judgement of the vestry for solution.

The poor were well provided for in Llantrisant. There was no heartless disregard of the sick as many people believe. A record for 20th September, 1809 states:—

> " *William Miles of Miskin and his wife were allowed five shillings relief during his illness.*"

These benefits were continued until the era of the great South Wales coalfields. The old parish vestry went so far as to make provision for death. In a meeting held at the Cross Keys on 29th February, 1804, Mr. David Jenkins, a shopkeeper, was bade to " furnish the paupers of this parish to the 1st May next with coffins of all sizes as it may happen, that is whenever a pauper died, to the time limited, shrouds included at a rate of 12s. 6d. each ". An incidental entry states:—

> " *Ordered to buy a sheet for the use of the parish, to dress out the corpses of the paupers, and to be left in the care of the Overseers of the Town Hamlet for the time being.*"

There was still some dishonesty among the officials who administered the funds. The Vestry discovered on 6th August, 1806, that " Thomas Jenkins detains the sum of £50 : 9s. : 10d., in his hand, of the money collected for relief of some of the poor in this parish ". Law action was to be taken if the money was not returned. By 1808, there was slackness in the administration. It was appointed, " that attendance of Ministers be optional " and there were also faults in appointing officials. They were often drawn by lottery and would be forced to accept the post and its financial loss. The appointed refused point blank or bribed themselves out of appointment, while others concealed their reluctance and got their own back by ill-treating the poor and making a profit. At a meeting on 7th June, 1809, at the Bear Inn, The Clerk, James Jacob, was " desired to write a letter to Edward Evan of Trideign and request immediately, without loss of time, to submit to the order of His Majesty's Justices of the Peace appointing him an Overseer of the Poor ".

The following selection of entries from the Parish Vestry records will show how the poor benefited, and how the children were used as apprentices and show that, for many in the locality, weaving and mat-making were the only trades:—

30th August, 1809:

Evan Williams, a weaver, was allowed £1 : 19s. : 0d. towards repairing " his weaving utensils and to buy some wool, in order that he may maintain his children and the whole of his weaving utensils belonging to his trade is to be entered on the parish book until he discharges his debt ".

25th April, 1810:

It was learnt that Thomas Harry was once more in circulation and he was granted 10s. " towards defraying the expenses for coming out of Cardiff Gaol, namely the fees to be paid to Mr. William Thomas Morgan, the gaoler, otherwise he could never come out to support himself or endeavour so to do ".

An agreement dated 15th May, 1812, confirmed the contract of David

Davies, surgeon, to serve the poor of the parish for £8 per year "with every medical assistance", and at the meeting on 20th May, a clothing allowance of £1 per child was granted to farmers for every child apprentice they engaged.

A local census was commissioned on 14th October, 1812 when Thomas Rimborn was ordered to take account of "all the houses in the town which the parish pay rent for". As a sequel to this survey, twenty-three occupiers of parish houses were ordered to quit on 21st October, 1812. It was also ordered that a search may be made after all who have deserted their families. The census was ordered because the Vestry found that they were supporting too many paupers and something like panic developed. The parish rate was fixed at nine shillings in the pound. It was directed on 4th November, 1812, "that the paupers who live singly are to be placed with others, and where there is no room or beds, to be placed in other rooms, where they can be placed in order to save the great expense the parish now pays for houses and fire", but on 3rd February, 1813, "all the paupers were able to bake in the workhouse oven gratis". The Overseers of the Poor seemed to have full control over each of their poor—"even to personal affairs. For some reason, it was ordered, "to stop William William's banns in the church next Sunday, and the Churchwardens and Overseers are desired to attend divine service for this purpose".

Llantrisant, like any other town, had its share of miscreants and complaints. An obvious shortcoming of the vestry system was that so much depended on the character of the official. On 5th December, 1810, Jennet Williams complained that "she has had no fire in her house this fortnight ago, and she owes 2s. 6d. for coal, and will not be trusted with any more until she pays the 2s. 6d.; the rain comes into her room and on her bed; she was promised a skirt and petticoat by the Rev. Mr. Pritchard, and she never had them; she has had no victuals in her house this day; she was allowed a sack of coal by the vestry and was refused it by David Arthur at the time".

Other entries were:—

> "*Richard Evans' wife was allowed 4s. to buy wool to make shirts for her children, also her son broke his limb lately and she applied to Mr. Harris for relief, which was refused to her at the time.*"

> "*Sarah Thomas, Nicholas's widow, applied to the Vestry for more clothes. She has only two old shirts, one old rug, one old blanket, one chaff pillow and she has no victuals in the house this evening and must be provided for immediately.*"

The question of cost still haunted the officials and in addition to this, there was rivalry between the hamlets in the parish and this had continued for a long period so that it was agreed on 3rd November, 1813, "to engage and divide the Paupers of the Five Hamlets in order that each hamlet may support and maintain themselves separately for one year from 1st February next". In the event of any disputes arising out of this arrangement, five respectable gentlemen and farmers would be called to form a committee to determine any dispute which may arise between the town, Gellywion, Miskin, Trane and Castellau.

In June 1813, bridges were wrecked and roads were made impassable and the Vestry was able to use the paupers to repair the bridges and roads. The Vestry was still in economic straits in September 1814 for an entry for 2nd September, records that " the Parishioners refused to pay their taxes ", and it was ordered that defaulters " will be proceeded against by law for the recovery ".

The administration became corrupt and inefficient. No care was taken over appointments and more often than not, people who did not have humanity in their make-up were appointed as officials. The following document was drawn up on 4th November, 1814. It is a damning document, which would nowadays rightly cause a riot:—

> " *We agree that lots be drawn for the children of Paupers fit and proper to be apprenticed upon the following terms:—that all the proper parties liable to take apprentices shall submit to take the person allotted; that in case of any person desirous of delivery, if they pay £5 to the Overseers of the Hamlet, the lot shall be drawn again and the £5 be paid, the person taking the child, and so on, until the child be settled, the additional sums to accompany the child, and it is considered that not any person shall be considered as liable to take a child unless he shall hold* £30 *per annum by the property tax.*"

The County Police Act was passed in 1839. The Quarter Sessions considered this Act but could not agree on the introduction of the police force for the whole county, though the court gave way to the pressure of the magistrates of the Lower Hundreds of Caerphilly and Miskin permitting them to introduce a small force of one Superintendent and six men for their own part of the County, which included Llantrisant as a town in the Miskin Hundred.

The first " Peelers " or police in Glamorgan date from 1839. The qualifications for appointment as Superintendent appeared in an advertisement in the " Cardiff and Merthyr Guardian " of 21st December, 1839. Among other things the applicant had to be under 40 years of age, stand 5 ft. 7 ins. without shoes, be able to read, write and keep accounts, be of strong constitution, free from bodily complaint and generally intelligent. Disqualified from appointment were gamekeepers, wood-rangers, bailiffs, parish clerks, hired servants or any person having any interest in any house for the retail of beer, wine and spirits. The extent of his district was detailed as Lower Miskin (parishes of Llantrisant, Pentyrch, Llantwit Fardre and Llanwonno) and Lower Caerphilly area. There is no mention of previous Police experience.

In January, 1840, a former member of the Metropolitan Police and then Sergeant at Haverfordwest, named Thomas Morgan Lewis, was appointed Superintendent, and shortly afterwards the six constables were sworn in. Of these six constables, one, James Hume, became the Llantrisant constable and lived on the Bull Ring. Superintendent Lewis, too, took up residence at Llantrisant though it has not been possible to find his name in the census returns for 1841. In November, 1841, the small local force was absorbed into the full County Force, Superintendent Lewis being given charge of the Newbridge (or Pontypridd) Division. James Hume became a Sergeant at Merthyr (in view of his previous police experience) and his place at Llantrisant was taken by P.C. Thomas Major, who was succeeded in 1844 by P.C. Thomas Williams. In 1848, Williams was replaced by P.C. Rees Rowlands, and, in 1848, Llantrisant became a Sergeant's Station. Sergeant John Thomas was previously stationed at Nelson and Newbridge and subsequently became a Superintendent at Merthyr Tydfil.

In 1871 the officer in charge was John French, who lived at the Police Station, Sir Davidstown. At one time the Police Station was located in Swan Street. The present Police Station was built in 1876. The officer at Llantrisant in 1884 was Sergeant William Hoyle and one of the Constables was Phillip Francis. The police arrangements for the safety of the crowd at the cremation of Dr. William Price was supervised by Superintendent Jones and Chief Constable Lindsey, who were assisted by Inspectors Jones of Pentre, Davies of Porth, Sergeant Hallett and a company of 50 Constables. This was perhaps their greatest achievement in maintaining order with crowds of upwards of 20,000 people present.

Early in the nineteenth century, coal was mined by Walter Coffin of Bridgend at Dinas in the Rhondda Valley. This marked the change from agriculture to industry and was one of the factors leading to the expansion of the district around Llantrisant. The surrounding countryside was known to abound in mineral wealth and several early iron works had been established. In the last 200 years there were several attempts to mine coal from numerous levels and pits. Among the earliest attempts were those made by Thomas Powell, Esq. One, the Trecastle Colliery, was not a flourishing concern but other levels, the Corporation Land Colliery, one near Beddau Station (now demolished) called Llantwit Walls End Colliery and others at Llantwit Fardre in 1839 proved successful. The first pit was sunk at Ddehewyd, a second one nearby on a site, which since 1913 is occupied by Trinity Chapel. A third pit Ystradberwig and a fourth at Ty'n-y-nant followed. In connection with the latter, Thomas Powell built Ida House and some offices of the pit. Subsequently the house became a small-holding but is now demolished. The house is commemorated by the name Heol Ida, Beddau. Thomas Powell died in 1863 and was succeeded by his sons, one of whom was also named Thomas Powell. He attempted to mine coal on Llantrisant Common about 1866 but these workings were abandoned.

These were the beginnings of the growth and development of the world-wide engineering firm, Powell Duffryn & Co. Ltd. This company is now amalgamated with three other companies, namely: Stephenson Clark, Corrals and Cory Bros.

The Powell Duffryn Company was formed with a capital of £500,000 in July, 1864, to acquire from the sons of the late Thomas Powell his collieries at Aberdare and in the Rhymney Valley. By 1947 when Britain's coal industry was nationalised, the Powell Duffryn Group's South Wales Collieries had become the largest single unit coal producing concern in the world, and the company owned the largest privately owned fleet of railway waggons in Britain. The company received £15.964,712 in compensation. Powell Duffryn is still a major power in the coal industry as wholesalers and retailers of coal. The company also has interests in shipping (Stephenson Clarke). Another associated company, Cory Bros. developed bunkering facilities throughout the world, operating in 46 countries. This company also has world-wide interests in oil, with a large installation at Barry. At Queensferry, Flintshire an automated mill makes fibreboard, which is increasingly used in the building industry. They also have an engineering works at Cardiff. A further development has been the manufacture of equipment for central heating and air conditioning.

Other speculators searched and found coal. In addition to the Llantwit Main Colliery Ltd. (1855) there was the Gelynog Llantwit Coal Company Ltd., who operated to the east and north of Llantrisant. To the south was probably the largest works—Cardiff Navigation Colliery (Coedcae & Lanelay) owned by T. J. Masters of Lanelay Hall. Loftus Terrace, Pontyclun, was owned by this company and provided accommodation for its work people. The houses were demolished in 1967. There was also the South Cambrian Colliery (closed 1915) owned by Ockwell Hawkins, Esq., M.E., of Llantrisant. Near Pontyclun, the Meiros Colliery Company operated. This site is now used by the local council for refuse disposal. All these works have long since closed. New speculations began at Coed Ely in 1901 when the first turf was cut. Sinking coal mines is a specialised work and strength and stamina are some of the attributes needed to carry out the work. This work brought men from other parts of the country. Work continued until the pit was sunk in 1909. After all the Llantwit Collieries had closed, a new colliery was sunk at Cwm, near Beddau, in 1909 and was ready for production by 1913.

In 1922, Ynysmaerdy Colliery was started by the Powell Duffryn Company but it was not until 1928 that the cages were installed in order to bring coal to the surface. This mine was never very successful, due particularly to the rock formation. A serious explosion occurred in the summer of 1941. This put the pit out of action and it has never resumed production. The latest coal mine to be opened in the area was at Llanharan in 1932 but this was closed in 1964 due to the policy of centralisation of the coal industry adopted by the National Coal Board. At the present time the Cwm Colliery at Beddau is the only colliery in full production. Even coal mined at Coed Ely is brought to the surface at Cwm. Coed Ely has an important coke oven plant. Drilling operations were made on Llantrisant Common recently in search of coal deposits.

Of the several iron works which have developed in the district during the last four hundred years, one of which was mentioned by Leland in 1538-40, only the Glamorgan Hematite Iron Ore Mine at Llanharry is still in production. The iron ore mine at Llanharry was started in 1901 and is the last of many small iron mines that were scattered throughout the area of South Wales. The only other mine, like that at Llanharry, is in Cumberland, where there is also unstratified hematite iron ore. The ore from Llanharry is sent by rail to Guest Keen Iron & Steel Works at Cardiff. The ore is mined by drilling holes with a pneumatic jack hammer fitted with an airleg which pushes the machine towards the rock face and holes thus drilled are then charged with explosive and fired at the end of the shift. A ventilating fan draws air down the shafts and discharges it, after passing through the workings up an incline from the 320 ft. level, where the fan is situated, to the surface. This removes all blasting fumes in time to permit the next shift to enter working places. A feature of the mine is that there is no benefaction or concentration of the ore on the surface and the miners have to exercise constant care when filling in. This has to be done therefore by hand shovelling, to ensure that stone or shale is not inadvertantly loaded with the ore. Since the mine is very wet, there is no dust problem and fortunately no gas escape occurs, hence some naked lights are still used. A 600 h.p. electric mine hoist works two cages, a steam winding engine for the second shaft. There are fitting, carpenter and blacksmith shops for repair and maintenance. The mine produces between 2,500 to 3,000 tons of ore a week, which contains about 50% metallic iron. The ore has low phosphorous, sulphur and silica content and can be used in the acid blast furnaces and can later be used to make good quality cast iron. Other works now closed down are the Trimsaron Coal & Iron Co. Ltd., and Mwyndy Iron Ore Co. Ltd., which was managed by William Vivian in the 1860's. This works was started in 1855 by R. Beaumont. The Bute Hematite Iron Ore Works (Dowlais Iron Co.) near Cefn-y-Parc Farm was started in 1852 and managed by Hussey Vivian, Esq. To the west of Llantrisant were the Tydu Iron Ore Works managed by Stephen Vivian, Esq., M.E. and the Loftus Iron Co. Ltd., Lanelay Colliery. The iron works were closely linked to coal pits because coal was used to smelt the iron when charcoal was replaced as a means of providing heat.

Quarrying was another important industry in the parish. Many quarries like those at Tylcha, Penycoedcae and Erw Hir are now closed, but Hendy Quarry, Miskin is still in production. It is interesting to remember that stone from this quarry was used to build the new road from Talbot Green to Ynysmaerdy in the 1920's.

11. The Dissolution of the Borough

With the passing of the Municipal Corporation Act of 1883, Llantrisant's status as a borough ended. The schedule to the Act stated that " Her Majesty has not been pleased to grant a charter to that place " and the property of the dissolved corporation of " The Constable of the Castle, Portreeve, Aldermen and Burgesses of Llantrisant " was supervised by the Charity Commission of England and Wales according to powers granted to this body by the 1883 Act. Due notice of the effects of the Act was given. The intentions of the Charity Commissioners were advertised on the 10th April, 1889 in the " Western Mail ", and the " South Wales Daily News ". A notice was put on the church door and officers of the corporation were notified.

The Commission ordered " That the following scheme be approved and established as the scheme for the application of the property of the late corporation, dissolved by the Municipal Corporations Act 1883 ". The scheme set up a body of thirteen competent persons, being Representative Trustees: but at first there shall be fifteen trustees. The trustees were to be elected to office for a term of five years in each case as follows:—

> " *Nine (hereinafter called Freemen's Trustees) by the persons whose names are for the time being on the Freeman's Roll.*"
> " *Three by the Vestry of the Parish of Llantrisant.*"
> " *One by the Cambrian Archaeological Association.*"

The scheme enabled the Trustees to apply for annual income of the Trust to defray the incidental and other expenses of the management and administration of the Trust, to maintain the Town Pump and any other improvement at Llantrisant subject to the approval of the Charity Commissioners. The scheme also stated that the mace and other effects, the charter and other documents mentioned in the Schedule to be deposited in some place in Llantrisant. The records are now in the Glamorgan Record Office. The Schedule was as follows:—

SCHEDULE

		Annual Value £	s.	d.
1.	Burgage rents in respect of waste lands held subject to a rent of £3 : 1s. : 7d. to the Marquis of Bute, amounting to (Not collected since 1875)	9	0	0
2.	Surface rights over the commons of Cymdda and Graig, containing 284 acres or thereabouts.			

3. A sum of £534:19s:8d. New Consols standing in the names of John Stuart Corbett, William Charles Luard (deceased), Evan John, and John Thomas.
4. Fees upon the admission of Freeman (average) 5 5 0
5. A Silver mace of the date A.D. 1633.
6. The charter, records and other documents.
7. A sum of £44: 19s.: 5d. cash.

Sealed by Order of the Board
this 17th day of December 1889.
G. H. Gauntlett.

The Town Trust was set up on the 17th December, 1889 in order to manage the Commons and exercise of pasture-rights. Under the Trust, the following rules and conditions had to be observed, and any person who offended against any of the following Bye-Laws would be proceeded against in court:—

" No person unless authorised by the Trustees shall:—

1. Affix any notice or advertisement in any part of the Town.
2. Not hold a political or religious demonstration on the lands of the Town.
3. Not damage or remove any landscape or property.
4. Cut grass or fern thereon for their own use.
5. Not deposit any refuse on the said lands.
6. Do any acts thereon which may be dangerous to person or animals.
7. Have entire horses or bulls over twelve months old on the lands.
8. Have swine over two months old on the lands.
9. Have animals suffering from any disease on the said land.
10. Search for game, except those entitled to the grazing rights.
11. The Trustees reserve the power to regulate the number of the Stock grazing on the said Lands and regulate the positions and portions of ground for grazing.
12. The Overseers or some authorised persons are empowered to remove or impound any animals not in accordance with these regulations; or any stray animals not being the property of persons entitled to the grazing rights on the said land."

There is, at the present time, a Royal Commission enquiring into the Rights and Customs of existing Common Lands. The Town Trust is still in being and the Court Leet is still held, but today it is done to perpetuate a custom and has become a social event. Likewise Freemen are still enrolled but this is only done to maintain an honourable tradition.

12. Doctor William Price (1800-1893)

William Price of Llantrisant is one of the most controversial figures of modern times. He was born on 4th March, 1800 in the Parish of Rudry, Caerphilly, the fifth child of Rev. William Price (1760-1841). He received his early education at Gatward's Day School, Machen and when he was thirteen years old, was apprenticed to Evan Edwards, a surgeon of Caerphilly. After studying at St. Bartholomew's Hospital, London, William Price was made a Licentiate of the Society of Apothecaries in September 1821 and in October, the same year, a Member of the Royal College of Surgeons. He was the youngest ever to be received as a Member of this institution.

In 1827, William Price made his home at Nantgarw, and became Medical Adviser to the Crawshay family and practised medicine at Pontypridd and Treforest. He built the Round Houses at Treforest.

Doctor Price was a vegetarian and a Chartist who, on one occasion, had to flee to France for safety. He also posed as a Druid and practised druidic rituals on the Rocking Stone at Pontypridd Common. Some of the older generation still remember the doctor dressed in his eccentric clothes, which consisted of a coat and trousers of green cloth and a red waistcoat, which had specially designed brass buttons with the image of his own goats printed on them. His headdress was a fox-skin, complete with tail. Dressed in this uniform he was a familiar sight riding about the parish in a pony and trap.

In 1884, Doctor Price was the centre of one of the more notable court cases of the day. He had been arrested by the local constable during the cremation ceremony of his son, to whom he had given the name Iesu Grist (Jesus Christ). This resulted in an appearance before the magistrate, at Pontypridd where local prejudice was shown against him. A further appearance took place before Judge Stephens at the Cardiff Assizes where William Price conducted his own defence. He was acquitted of the charge against him, that of burning his son, on the payment of one farthing costs. By this judgement, cremation was thus established as a legal practice for the first time. This trial was featured on BBC television in June 1965 in a series spotlighting prominent trials in Wales and was entitled " Invitation to a Burning ". Harlech Television has screened a dramatic version on the life of Dr. Price in 1972, and a stage production entitled " Celtic Fire " was performed at the Casson Studio Theatre by the Welsh Theatre Company in Cardiff.

When William Price died on 23rd January, 1893 at Ty'r Clettwr, he was himself cremated on 31st January at East Caerlan field. The event created great interest and there were over 20,000 people in the town to witness the ceremony. The service was conducted by Rev. D. Fisher, Curate of Llantrisant assisted by Rev. J. Williams of Pontyclun, who read an adaptation of the service appointed for " The Burial of the

Dead at Sea ", in which the words of committal used on this occasion were: " Yr ym ni yn rhoddi ei gorph i'r tan gan ddisgwyl am adgfodiad y meirw ac am fywyd y byd y sydd ar ddyfod ", etc. The form of service had been approved by the Bishop of the Diocese. The preparations for the cremation began with bringing coal and wood to the site and fencing off an area away from the crowds. The iron coffin was brought on a horse-driven hearse by Edgar G. Mathews, Esq., who worked for Wilks & Powis of Pontypridd. They were also Contractors for the Masters family of Lanelay Hall.

After the religious service had ended the fire was lit. At 3.30 p.m. the coffin was withdrawn from the flames. Afterwards many from the crowd in the field became souvenir hunters. Several people are the proud possessors of pieces of the iron coffin. Other souvenirs which have come down to us are coloured postcards showing Dr. Price in his colourful costume and composite pictures entitled " In Memoriam 1893 ". The " In Memoriam " photograph was a reproduction of photographs on headscarves which were also on sale at Llantrisant.

Dr. William Price still arouses much interest and discussion and in September 1947 a brass tablet was unveiled at Zoar Chapel, Llantrisant, which now stands on the site of Ty Clettwr, where he died. Miss Penelopen Price, the doctor's daughter, performed the unveiling ceremony. The ceremony was sponsored by the National Cremation Society of Britain. Miss Price resided at East Caerlan in a house near the site of the first public cremation. Dr. Price's son, Nicholas, died in June 1963 and was cremated at Glyntaff, Treforest which was the first crematorium in Wales.

Miss Penelopen Price, the daughter of Dr. Price resided at East Caerlan. On 8th October, 1966, at the North Chapel Crematorium, Glyntaff, Treforest, near Pontypridd, Miss Price unveiled stained glass windows as a memorial to her father who legalised cremation in 1884. The windows are beautiful to look at and have some interesting symbols. The main central window depicts the Resurrected and Ascended Christ with arms outstretched in a beckoning attitude. Surmounting the figure is shown the symbol of the Holy Spirit in the form of the Dove. The left and right hand windows depict symbols of the Resurrection. The left hand window shows the Phœnix rising again from its own ashes signifying Resurrection and the fact that those who fall asleep in Christ shall rise again to newness of life. The right hand window shows the Peacock symbolising immortality and is derived from an old legend that the Peacock's flesh is incorruptible. In like manner Our Lord's body did not see corruption, but was raised up glorified on the third day. So also does He raise up all true believers to a more glorious existence. The symbols shown in the left circular tracery section is the Butterfly symbolising Eternal Life through Christ and the right circular tracery section has the Easter Lily because it blooms at Eastertide and is the symbol of Our Lord's Resurrection.

Miss Penelopen Price died in October 1977 aged 91 years old and was cremated at Glyntaff Crematorium, Treforest.

HOMAGE TO DOCTOR WILLIAM PRICE, LLANTRISANT

Tune: God Bless the Prince of Wales.
Words: Gwilym Llaeron (William John Lewis).

Today we sing the praises
Of Dr. William Price,
Who legalised cremation
Throughout the British Isles.
His infant he cremated
One day at East Caerlan,
And thereby gained the hatred
Of almost all in Llan.

Chorus.

So let us sing the praises
Of this farsighted man,
Who legalised cremation,
That day at East Caerlan.

And here on the Bullring
In sight of East Caerlan,
Today we place a statue,
In honour of this man,
He was a Welsh Heretic
A queer sort of chap,
His deed that day set firmly
Llantrisant on the map.

He also was a Druid
And Chartist of renown,
This character made headlines
In cities and in town,
Dressed in a quaint regalia
His cap made out of fur,
When riding through the area
He always caused a stir.

And here we are gathered
Today as you can see,
To place this fine memorial
Up to his memory,
So let us raise our voices
In song up to the skies,
And thank the Lord for sending
Us, Dr. William Price.

These words were sung at the unveiling of the statue to Dr. Wm. Price in the Bull Ring, Llantrisant on Monday, 3rd May, 1982 in the presence of the Mayor, Councillor George Preston and the Mayoress Mrs. Preston.

13. The Lord Mayor of London at Llantrisant

During 1965, the Parish Church at Llantrisant has undergone its first major reconstruction for 72 years. One of the events connected with the reconstruction of 1893 was an occasion which proved to be a highlight and memorable event for all who witnessed it. The special day was 4th July, 1892, when the Lord Mayor of London, Sir David Evans, K.C.M.G., D.L., F.R.G.S., visited Llantrisant on the occasion of his state visit to South Wales. After arriving at Cardiff he went to Bridgend, where he witnessed an eisteddfod. His visit to Llantrisant is recorded in the Parish Magazine, July 1892:—

The visit of the Lord Mayor of London to his native town of Llantrisant on the 4th July is an event to be remembered in the history of the Parish, and one that deserves more than a passing notice. The hundreds, not to say thousands, that thronged the roads and streets on that eventful day and the triumphal arches and flags and mottoes, and the shouts and songs of welcome, that greeted his Lordship as he made his way from the Great Western Railway Station up to the Old Bull Ring (a relic of the manners and customs of a past generation), in the centre of the town, showed that someone was coming whom the people delighted to honour. It was, indeed, no small matter for the inhabitants of a little Welsh town like this to see one of their own kinsmen, holder of the highest civic office in the greatest city in the world, coming back to his native village, indeed to the very playground of his boyhood, wearing the splendid robes and golden chain of a Lord Mayor of London. The following was the order:—

ORDER OF PROCESSION

Llantrisant Drum and Fife Band.

Carriage drawn by goats.

Sunday School Children:—

No. 1 *Established Church*
2 *Welsh Methodists*
3 *English Wesleyans*
4 *English Methodists*
5 *Bible Christians*
6 *Baptists*
7 *Congregationalists*

Cymmer Brass Band.

Freemen and Inhabitants of Town Friendly Societies:—

No. 1 *Forests*
2 *Ivorites*
3 *Grand United Order of Oddfellows*
4 *M.U. Oddfellows* (*Bute Lodge*)

Public Bodies: —

Members of Board of Guardians
Members of Llantrisant School Board
Members of Llantrisant Town Trust
40 *boys mounted on Ponies*

Mounted Police	*The Right Honourable The Lord Mayor Carriages.*	*Mounted Police*

When the front part of the procession reached the Bull Ring, a large circle was formed, leaving a space in the middle for the Lord Mayor's carriage to drive through; and then the school children led by Mr. W. Davies and accompanied by the Cymmer Brass Band, struck up a song specially composed by Mr. Fardo, the Postmaster of Cardiff. It was sung to the familiar tune of " God Bless the Prince of Wales " and was soon taken up by a great part of the assemblage. The words of the refrain after each verse are now very familiar to nearly all the inhabitants of the town and neighbourhood: —

" Llantrisant from her mountains
Smiles o'er Morganwg's vales,
And sends to mighty London
A real Lord Mayor from Wales."

As soon as the Lord Mayor's carriage had drawn up in the centre of the Bull Ring, the following address was presented to him: —

TO THE RIGHT HONOURABLE DAVID EVANS, LORD MAYOR OF LONDON

We, the undersigned, on behalf of the inhabitants of the Town and Parish of Llantrisant, desire to give your Lordship a hearty welcome to this your native place.

We have already, on a recent occasion, offered you our warm congratulations on your attainment of the exalted position which you now hold, and we then ventured to express a hope that your tenure of that high office would bring honour to yourself, your office, and your native land. We are glad to note, from many indications, that those hopes seem likely to be fulfilled. We appreciate very highly the feeling that seems to animate you and to knit you with indissoluble bonds to our common Fatherland—" Cas gwr no charo'r wlad a'i mago ". And we rejoice to think that your object in coming here today is not only to meet once more many old friends of your boyhood, but also to lend a helping hand for the restoration of the tower of our ancient Parish Church, whose sweet-toned bells have sounded in the ears of our ancestors for many and many a generation.

We welcome you to our midst, we thank you for your presence, and we wish you every happiness and prosperity for the future.

The Lord Mayor replied in a cordial and vigorous speech, which was warmly and repeatedly applauded, and then drove on towards the National Schools to open the Bazaar in aid of the Parish Church,

Tower, Bells, etc. After leaving the Bazaar, the procession was reformed and proceeded with the Lord Mayor as far as the Cymdda Bach, on the road to Pontypridd.

The bazaar which was opened at the National Schools by the Lord Mayor realised the sum of £400. This was devoted to the restoration fund for work carried out on the tower and bells in 1893.

At Pontypridd Sir David Evans took part in the Proclamation Ceremony at the Rocking Stone, on the Common. This was to herald the 1893 South Wales Eisteddfod. The custom of proclaiming the Eisteddfod is still performed annually.

Sir David Evans was born on 21st April, 1849 the son of Thomas Evans, Glanmychydd. After attending a local school he went to Merton, Surrey and later completed his education in France. In 1868 he took a leading position in the firm of Messrs. Richard Evans & Co. Silk Merchants and Trimming Manufacturers, Watling Street, London. He had been an Alderman of the old Borough and a Trustee of the Town Trust.

1870	*Made Freeman of Llantrisant*
1874	*Elected to the Court of Common Council*
1883	*Elected Alderman of Llantrisant Borough*
1884	*Elected Alderman of City of London*
1885-6	*Senior Sheriff of London and Middlesex*
1891	*Elected Lord Mayor of London*

In addition to the above honours, David Evans, D.L., F.R.G.S., was a Justice of the Peace for the County of Glamorgan and the County of Surrey.

At the time of his election to Lord Mayor, Sir David Evans lived at Ewell Grove, Ewell, Surrey with his wife and family. He had married a Miss Boakes of Kent. To mark the honour bestowed on a native of Llantrisant, a deputation consisting of J. Treharne, Esq., E. Treharne, Esq., Samuel Evans, Esq., J.P., Tregerig, Dr. Morgan, "Morien" and Rev. J. P. Hughes, Vicar of Llantrisant attended on the new Lord Mayor and an address was presented to him by Evan John, Esq., J.P.

On the 30th July, 1892, Queen Victoria appointed David Evans a Knight Commander of the Most Distinguished Order of St. Michael and St. George.

Further honour was to come. On Thursday, 17th November, 1892, a resolution was passed by the Court of Common Council recording the honourable and eventful year of office of Sir David Evans. A Testimonial Fund was opened and the result was the "Welsh National Presentation" held in London in December 1892. Sir J. H. Puleston, M.P. presented Lady Evans with a portrait and Sir David received an Oriental gold service. Sir David had brought great credit to the City of London and to Wales. He is commemorated in Llantrisant by having a street, Sir David's Place and Davidstown named after him. Road improvements were made in Sir David's Place for the first time in 1965.

14. Modern Times

By the end of the nineteenth century, people were taking greater interest in national and local affairs. All ratepayers were now entitled to vote and they wished to govern their own districts. Two Acts of Parliament, the Local Government Acts of 1888 and 1894 were responsible for organising efficient supervision of each district. By the 1888 Act, County and Borough Councils were established and the Act of 1894 established Urban, Rural District and Parish Councils. By these Acts, the Parish Vestry lost what remained of its authority and is now only concerned with church matters. The Llantrisant and Llantwit Fardre Rural District was originally part of the Pontypridd Union Rural Sanitary Authority, which comprised Eglwysilan, Llanfabon, Llantrisant, Llantwit Fardre, Llanwonno, Pontypridd and Rhondda.

The first elections for the Llantrisant and Llantwit Fardre Rural District Council were held on 17th December, 1894 and the first Council elected was as follows:—

Town Ward

Godfrey L. Clark, J.P., gentleman; Evan John, J.P., gentleman; Stephen Vivian, mining engineer.

Tonyrefail Ward

E. S. Richards, mining engineer; J. S. Williams, colliery manager; Wm. Evans, farmer.

Llantwit Fardre

Thos. Lewis, grocer; Daniel Bryant, postmaster; Lewis Williams, schoolmaster.

The first Chairman was Godfrey L. Clark, J.P. of Talygarn House, High Sheriff of Glamorgan.

The following names are members of the first Parish Council also elected on 17th December, 1894:—

Town (South Ward)

Charles Cooksley, builder; Thos. John, farmer; Philip John Dunn, gentleman; Rev. J. P. Hughes, vicar; John Morgan, builder; Evan Lewis, farmer; Wm. John, collier; Lewis Ajax, collier.

Tonyrefail (North Ward)

Isaac Owen, schoolmaster; Wm. Williams, colliery manager; Evan Thomas, gentleman; Robert Evans, collier; Thos. Thomas, check weigher; David Rowlands, collier; David Naunton Morgan, surgeon.

To form the district council, the Parish of Llantrisant as it was in 1894 and the Parish of Llantwit Fardre were amalgamated: —

Llantrisant	:	14,209 acres
Llantwit Fardre	:	4,224 acres
Total area	:	18,433 acres

This authority was one of the largest of its kind in Britain. The number of councillors has doubled since the original election to 18 members who represent an estimated population of 27,680. The Council is responsible for providing houses, recreational facilities, lighting and similar services and the repair of by-roads, trimming of hedges etc. Laws passed by the National Government known as "statutory" laws are carried out in practice by the local authority while "mandatory" laws may be carried out at the option of the local authority. By this system, each locality is governed in a democratic way, laws being observed and bye-laws passed by a representative body elected by the people.

The last officers of the L.R.D.C. were: —

Clerk to the Council:	*W. I. Maddocks, Esq.*
Engineer & Surveyor:	*T. J. Hopkins, B.Sc.*
Treasurer & Accountant:	*R. J. Brown, F.I.M.T.A., D.P.A.*
Medical Officer of Health:	*Dr. Eileen G. Watkins, M.B., B.Ch., B.A.O., D.P.H., L.M. (R.O.T.)*

The Chief Officer of the new Taff-Ely Borough Council was Geoffrey Hockin, Esq., BA. He was the former Clerk to the Llantrisant Rural District Council. Mr. Hockin died in January 1982 while still in office. The first Mayor was Mr. Winslade Roderick, Tonyrefail, who has been a council member for the last 36 years.

The first meeting of the new District Council was held in the Parish Offices, Llantrisant, on 11th January, 1895. The 60th anniversary dinner of this meeting was held on 11th January, 1955. At the final dinner of the District Council, the last Chairman, Leslie Carter, Esq., J.P., presented guests with a commemorative plate bearing the Council Coat of Arms and dated 1895-1974.

At Local Government Reorganisation, Llantrisant was represented on the Glamorgan County Council by: —

County Alderman William John Lewis, J.P., Beddau
County Councillor Kelvin Eason, Llantrisant

Beddau, which is in the Town Ward had the distinction of providing the Chairman of both the County Council and Llantrisant Council for the year 1966-67: —

Chairman, Glamorgan County Council:
County Alderman Theophilus Griffiths

Chairman, Llantrisant and Llantwit Fardre Rural District Council:
Councillor Glyn Phillips

During a dinner to mark the end of the County Council, members were presented with a stainless steel goblet bearing the County Council Coat of Arms and dated 1889-1974.

The new Mid-Glamorgan County Council came into being on 1st April, 1974, and the Town Ward of Llantrisant is represented by:—

Councillor Kelvin Eason, Llantrisant
Councillor Tudor John, Llantrisant
Councillor Luther Lodwig, Church Village
Councillor Mrs. Alice Tyrrell, Llantwit Fardre

The present members representing the Town Ward on the Taff-Ely Borough Council from 1st April, 1974, are:—

Councillor Stanley G. Balby, Talbot Green
Councillor David J. Harrison, Talbot Green
Councillor Cyril J. Hurley, Talbot Green
Councillor Watcyn R. Jacob, Beddau
Councillor Tudor John, Llantrisant
Councillor George Preston, Llantrisant
Councillor Kenneth W. Roderick, Pontyclun

The Parish Offices continue to play a part in the administration of the district. The new Llantrisant Community Council will have its headquarters here. The Community Council replaces Llantrisant Parish Council formed in 1895. The last members of the Parish Council were:—

David Mostyn Brooks, Tonyrefail
Evelyn Enid Bunston, Pontyclun
Frederick Croad, Tonyrefail
Patrick Francis Doyle, Talbot Green
Edwin George Edmunds, Tonyrefail
Denzil Mordecai Edwards, Talygarn
Edward Evans, Tonyrefail
Oswald Howard George, Tonyrefail
Cyril John Hurley, Talbot Green
John Warren Kiff, Talbot Green
Bleddyn Gordon Miles, Llantrisant
Barrie Nobel Pickins, Gilfach Goch
George Preston, Llantrisant
Vernon Pullin, Tonyrefail
Alec James Ridley, Tonyrefail

From 1st April, 1974, the first members of the new Llantrisant Community Council are:—

Chairman: *Evelyn Enid Bunston, Pontyclun*
Arthur Applegate, Tonyrefail
Jack Daughters, Gilfach Goch
Edwin George Edmonds, Tonyrefail

The Author presents a copy of his book written for the Investiture Celebrations in 1969 to Col. Traherne of Castellau Fawr while Rev. E. Davies, Vicar of Llantrisant looks on

Llantrisant Town Hall. Monday, 2nd June, 1980. Opening the "Ridgeway Walk"—through Llantrisant—unveiling by Sir Cennydd Traherne K.G., Mayor of Taff Ely, Mayoress Mrs. Davies, High Sheriff, Chairman of Leisure Committee: Mr. David Jones

Llantrisant Court Leet, Friday. 6th June, 1980. Sir Brandon Rhys-Williams (Chairman), Cledwyn Jones (Clerk) with Trustees

Llantrisant Town Trust. Court Leet—Making of Freemen, Friday, 6th June, 1980.

Llantrisant Town Mace dating from 1633

Loving Cup presented by Sir Brandon Rhys-Williams to the Freemen of Llantrisant

Members of the Pontyclun Teachers' Association at Blackpool. March 1978 with Mr. Dewi G. Bonner and Mrs. Margaret Bonner attending a dinner given by Welsh Delegates to Conference

Our photograph shows the well-known and popular Llantrisant Male Choir outside the Royal Albert Hall in April 1979. They were appearing in the 1,000 Voices Concert organised by the South Wales Association. Several Llantwit-Fardre parishioners are members of the choir conducted by George Mountford.

Miss Jeannetta Thomas — 112 years old. Oldest person ever recorded to live in Britain. Miss Thomas was in business at Commercial Street, Tynant.

Born Llantrisant, 2nd December, 1869. Celebrated 112th birthday Wednesday, 2nd December, 1981. Died Southways, Cowbridge, Tuesday, 4th January, 1982. Buried at Cefn Parc Cemetery, Llantrisant on Friday, 22nd January, 1982.

Miss Jeannetta Thomas at Southways, Cowbridge celebrating her 112th birthday on Wednesday, 2nd December, 1981 with Councillor & Mrs. George Preston, Mayor, Mayoress of Borough of Taff Ely and Mrs. Doreen Powell, Chairperson of Llantrisant Community Council and Community Councillors, Dillwyn Lewis, Morgan Lewis, Edward Evans, Mrs. Evelyn Bunston and Mrs. Annie Herbert

County Alderman William John Lewis, J.P., Beddau. Gwilym Llaeron, poet

A view, taken 1982, from Y Felin Wynt of New Park, Talbot Green, showing the Tesco Superstore which opened in November 1979

Vice Chairman: *Edward Evans, Tonyrefail*
John Hendy, Beddau
Clifford Hughes, Beddau
Douglas John Jacka, Gilfach Goch
John Jones, Gilfach Goch
Geoffrey Paul Lake, Llantrisant
Eirlys Lewis, Talbot Green
Morgan Lewis, Talbot Green
Doreen Powell, Tonyrefail
Vernon Pullin, Tonyrefail
Alec James Ridley, Tonyrefail

The first major undertaking of the new District Council was the provision of a new Water Supply. This was recorded in the Llantrisant Church Monthly in June 1896:—

> "*The month of May 1896 will be long remembered in the annals of Llantrisant as that in which the new supply of water, brought in iron pipes from the hills four or five miles above the town reached Llantrisant, to the great relief of the inhabitants, who have in many cases been greatly inconvenienced by the drought that has prevailed for many weeks. It is true that the water has so far been considerably discoloured by the tar, etc., with which the pipes appear to have been lined, but it is hoped that all discolouration from this cause will soon cease, and that then the water will be as clear and pure when it reaches Llantrisant as it is said to be when it enters the pipes in the hills. The Llantrisant and Llantwit Fardre District Council are to be congratulated upon the completion of their water supply scheme, which promises to prove a very great and lasting benefit to Llantrisant, Tonyrefail, Gilfach and the neighbourhood generally.*"

In addition to the setting up of the new administration, the nineties were a period of great expansion in the parish of Llantrisant. Socially, much time was devoted to concerts, sales of work and teas which were the means of fund-raising for projects in the town in 1892. Money was needed for the restoration of the Church tower and re-setting the bells. During this work a baptistry was installed. This white marble baptistry was first used on Thursday, 4th November, 1897, when Miss Grace Williams was baptised by Rev. Daniel Fisher.

Llantrisant has always been noted for the large number of public houses. In 1871 they were listed as:—

Angel: *George Bowen, High Street*
Brynteg Arms: *Mrs. Mary Jones, Newbridge Road*
**Butcher's Arms*: *James Carter, Sarn Street*
**Cross Inn*: *James Evans, Cross Inn*
**Cross Keys*: *Robt. Griffiths, High Street*
Fox & Hounds: *Ann Roberts, Commercial Street*

George: *David Morgan, Swan Street*
Greyhound: *Charles Davies, Llantrisant*
Horse & Groom: *Thomas David, Commercial Street*
Llantrisant Inn: *Thomas John, Sarn Street*
**New Inn*: *Samuel Spencer, Llantrisant*
Rickards Arms: *Richard Evans, Swan Street*
Rock Fountain: *Phillip Rowe, Swan Street*
Shrewsbury Arms: *John Hughes, Commercial Street*
**Wheatsheaf Inn*: *Roderick Lewis, Llantrisant*
White Hart: *Mrs. Mary Ann Davies, High Street*
*—open at the present time.

Other inns, now closed, were:—

The Colliers, Penygawsi
Mount Pleasant, Commercial St.
Castle Inn, St. Davidstown
Welcome Inn, Heol Sarn

There were also four beer retailers:—

Thomas Edwards, St. Davidstown
J. Willis, Sarn Street
Wm. Giles, Penygawsi
Henry Gibbon, Castle Mynach

A new hostelry will open shortly in Penygawsi called 'The Penny Farthing'.

Inns found a ready custom in this industrial area but beer drinking was not the only leisure pursuit. Llantrisant had many clubs and societies. The Llantrisant Rugby Club started its long career in the 1880's. There was the Temperance Society, which started in 1885. The Angel Inn (now known as the 'Pwysty') was famous for its large Ball Court where many a sporting challenge was accepted and settled. The game was played until the early years of this century. There was also a flourishing Quoit Club of 40 members. The Good Templars (94 members) were engaged on "useful and enduring work". During the winter of 1896 a Young Men's Club was started. A gymnasium was set up at the National Schools and a reading room at the Town Hall. There was an entrance fee of 1s. and subscriptions were 3d., in advance, each Saturday. The aims of the club were summed up in the club motto: "Mens sana in corpore sano" (a healthy mind in a healthy body). The Church Lad's Brigade for boys 14 to 19 years was started. The qualifications of entry were as follows:—

1. *To be a member of a Bible Class or a Sunday School.*
2. *To be a total abstainer.*
3. *To be within the age limit.*
4. *To pay an entrance fee of half-a-crown and a subscription of 3d. per week.*

It was these various organisations led by the Parish Church, that held functions to raise the required funds for the National Schools extension or any other charitable cause in the parish. Much of this work was organised and carried out by the gentry of the district. Patrons of the School Bazaar (1897) were:—

Lady Windsor, St. Fagan's Castle
Lady Price-Fothergill, Hensol Castle

Mrs. Godfrey L. Clark, Talygarn
Mrs. Kay, The Elms, Llantrisant
Mrs. Gwilym Williams, Miskin Manor
Mrs. Williams, Henstaff Court
Miss B. Tandy, Broadlands, Bridgend

An annual occasion for celebration was St. David's Day:—

1896 *A Pink and White Tea and Concert*
1897 *Japanese Tea and Concert*
1898 *Welsh Tea and Waxwork Exhibition and Concert. The Llantrisant Male Voice Party took part.*

Each year an idea or theme was adopted and this added to the interest of the event. This record of the appearance of the Llantrisant Male Voice Choir in March 1898 is the only record of the choir, which existed during the period of 1888-1898. Owing to the policies of the conductors during the nineteenth century to be responsible for all the affairs of the choir, no records were kept.

The present Llantrisant Male Voice Party was formed in 1909 when the first conductor was C. Davies Esq., a railway signalman. In 1912 he was transferred to Abertillery by the Railway Company and therefore resigned from the conductorship. He was succeeded by Jenkin Thomas, Esq., of Miskin, who was by trade a hay and corn merchant. In August 1923 he was succeeded by Luther Jones, Esq. During the period of its existence the choir has given 835 concerts (1909-1965), for charity and has raised £4,055 for a variety of worthy causes. The first annual dinner took place at the Craig-y-nos Hotel in October, 1959, to celebrate the choir's Golden Jubilee. In May 1965, the choir made a memorable and distinguished contribution to the Beddau centenary celebrations. The choir has been fortunate to have such loyal members over the years and in particular faithful and sterling service has been rendered by the accomplished musicianship of Mrs. Lottie Williams who was accompanist to the choir 1919-1960. Another such member was the secretary, E. O. Cole, Esq. (1923-1961), who was made a life member of the choir, for services rendered on its behalf. Luther Jones, Esq., was honoured in 1973 with a presentation dinner to mark his 50 years as conductor.

Mr. Jones died at his home in Cross Inn in June 1974. The Choir continues to give pleasure to a wide circle of people. In 1939 Llantrisant was featured in the Paul Robeson film "Proud Valley", which portrayed musical life in a Welsh village. Llantrisant has many distinguished singers in recent years, Gwynneth Morgan, Jennie Nicholas and Eric Lewis. In 1974 Jeffrey Hooper has appeared in "New Faces", "Opportunity Knocks," and "Golden Shot" on T.V. with distinction, and has made his first recordings for E.M.I.

During this period Llantrisant boasted a Drum and Fife Band, a stringed band, which, together with Miss E. Bowen's Gipsy Chorus, entertained the people. Also Llantrisant was the venue of several Eisteddfodau. Amid all this activity additional opportunity was given to all to further their education. Llantrisant had evening classes in the National Schools in 1898 when the enrolling fee was two shillings.

One of the most memorable events in Llantrisant was the celebration of Queen Victoria's Jubilee. A programme of events was arranged but some thought was also given to a permanent memorial. At first it was thought to install a clock in the Church Tower but this was not to be. It was proposed by Godfrey L. Clark, Esq., J.P., High Sheriff of Glamorgan, Talygarn that a Children's Convalescent Home be set up at "The Rest", Porthcawl. This idea was taken up and became a practical and useful reality. The town was gaily decorated with mottoes and bunting and was blessed with fine weather. The school was closed for a week. A generous inhabitant of the town provided a tea in the Vicarage grounds. After a short service in the Parish Church, at 3.30 p.m., the Sunday School marched to the Vicarage grounds, headed by the Llanharan Brass Band. After tea, there were games, swings and races. In the evening, hundreds of people went to the Graig to watch the bonfire which had been erected in West-Caerlan. At 10 p.m. the bonfire was lit by Master Norman Hughes (the Vicarage) and Master Dunn of Crofta. Forty bonfires were to be seen from West-Caerlan that evening.

The next day, The Parish Church Welsh Choir went to the Diamond Jubilee Festival held at Llandaff Cathedral. An interesting event which can be seen in a photograph was held on Wednesday 30th June 1897:—

> "*About seventy-five of the old inhabitants of this ancient borough over 65 years of age were invited to a dinner to celebrate the Diamond Jubilee of our Queen. An excellent spread was prepared for them at the Town Hall. The old people were delighted with the treat, during which they were entertained with songs, quartettes, etc. Before they left each one had a card given him, beautifully illuminated, in memory of Her Majesty's illustrious reign. After singing "God Save the Queen" they left the room and a photograph of the whole party was taken under the ruins of the old castle.*"

Teas were given to the children. The Masters family of Lanelay Hall entertained over 900 children to tea and each one received a penny before leaving for home. Mrs. Clark of Talygarn presented the Jubilee medals.

At Talygarn House, the children of the Pontypridd Union and Cottage Homes were entertained to tea and listened to the Llanharan Brass Band. After some firework displays each child received a bun before leaving for Pontypridd.

At Miskin, the village had been beautifully decorated with three noble arches of ivy, which spanned the road fronting the lodge gates. On the arches were the red and white letters: VICTORIA. Here at the Manor, children of the village were entertained to tea and sports and each child received a Jubilee medal from Judge Gwilym Williams.

At Beddau, tea and games were also arranged and a collection made towards the cost of a Harmonium. This "Jubilee Harmonium" was used for the first time on Sunday, 1st August, 1897 at 2.30 when Rev. Daniel Fisher conducted a service and delivered a most impressive address on the occasion.

When the twentieth century dawned life continued in the usual day-to-day trend. Fund-raising activities continued but now these funds were raised for soldiers fighting in the Boer War. In 1900, Llantrisant Parish was much larger than at present and included the Parishes of Pontyclun, Llanharan, Llanwonno, Ystradfodwg (Rhondda), Gilfach Goch and Tonyrefail. Llantwit Fardre (Church Village) was linked to Pentyrch but the living was under the patronage of the Vicar of Llantrisant. At this time the Parish had seven curates, two lay readers and five unpaid lay readers to attend to approximately 20,000 people. The Parish was twelve miles from end to end and had an area of 16,000 acres. When a petition was circulated against Disestablishment of the Welsh Church, 2,182 signatures were gathered from the Parish. In fifteen years prior to 1900, the Parish had built seven new churches and two new mission rooms. To pay for further expansion, the Llantrisant Centenary Fund was started with an appeal for £5,000. The money was needed for a new church at Tonyrefail, to clear debts on churches, mission room and two National Schools (£1,400) and for further sub-division of this large parish.

The new Llantrisant Rural District Council was anxious to improve and widen the roadway leading from Swan Street to the Allt. This involved an arrangement whereby the churchyard was extended and a "substantial boundary wall along the new boundary line". This was necessary if more graves were to be opened in the churchyard. It was becoming quite full and another cemetery would be needed soon. The new extensions to the churchyard delayed the need for a new cemetery until 1918 when Cefn Parc Cemetery was opened. This is administered by the Llantrisant Community Council.

Llantrisant continued to mark, with special celebrations, the national events of coronations, war and peace, but on 7th August, 1902, the Marquess of Bute who was also Lord of the Borough came of age. All children under 14 years of age were entertained to a tea party. A deputation from Llantrisant presented the Marquess of Bute with an illuminated address at Cardiff Castle on Monday, 4th August, 1902:—

TO THE MOST HON. THE MARQUESS OF BUTE,
EARL OF DUMFRIES, EARL OF WINDSOR,
BARON CARDIFF OF CARDIFF

"The Freemen and Inhabitants of the small but ancient town of Llantrisant, whose castle has for centuries belonged to your Lordship's ancestors, and with whose history your family has been honourably connected for so many years, desire to take the present opportunity of tendering your Lordship their hearty congratulations upon the attainment of your majority, and to express the hope that you may long be spared to fulfil the duties to which your high position and rare opportunities seem to call you.

" They remember with gratitude the many benefits that your family have conferred upon their town in the past, and especially they would call to mind the Educational benefits conferred by your Grandfather and Father upon the inhabitants of Llantrisant, and though their town has in recent years been shorn of much municipal dignity, they recall with pride the fact that your ancestors for many generations held the hereditary office of Lord of the Borough of Llantrisant.

" Praying that the blessing of Almighty God may rest upon you both in your public and your private life,

" We are, on behalf of the Freemen and Inhabitants of Llantrisant

" Signed J. PRITCHARD HUGHES (vicar of Llantrisant), Chairman of the Meeting.

EVAN JOHN, Chairman of the Town Trust.

TALIESIN MORGAN, Clerk of the Town Trust ".

Also at this time Edward VII's coronation was held (9th August) and on the occasion of the ending of the Boer War (2nd June, 1902) a Union Jack was flown from the Church Tower.

Most projects were halted by World War I. The twenties brought a period of expansion in industry and building. The Llantrisant Rural District Council was empowered to build houses and several schemes were started at Beddau 1921-25, Pontyclun 1925 onwards, and at Penygawsi (Head of the Causeway) in 1936. About 1930 Llantrisant Park was completed but this is now under reconstruction due to the building of a new swimming pool which has cost £75,000. Transport began to be organised and now formed the pattern of life as we know it today.

On Tuesday, 17th December, 1968, Her Majesty Queen Elizabeth visited Llantrisant to open the new Royal Mint. She was accompanied by the Duke of Edinburgh and the Prince of Wales.

The Mint at Llantrisant is used to manufacture the new Decimal coinage producing the ½p, 1p and 2p decimal " coppers ". The complete change-over to decimal coinage took place on 15th February, 1971.

Interest in decimal currency in this country goes back at least to 1824 when an M.P. introduced a motion favouring a change. Since then there have been several committees or commissions to consider the subject, the first decimal coin, the florin being introduced in 1849. The U.S.A. was the first modern state to adopt a decimal currency in 1792 and France followed in 1793. Details of the new system embodied in the Decimal Currency Act were given in a Government White Paper published in December 1966:—

Decimal Day—15th February, 1971.

Complete changeover: 1975.

The halfpenny was withdrawn 1st August, 1969.

The half crown was withdrawn end of 1969.

All new coins carry on the obverse, the portrait of Her Majesty The Queen by Mr. Arnold Mackin, O.B.E., R.A. The reverse designs from $\frac{1}{2}$p to 10p are by Mr. Christopher Ironside.

On 25th April, 1967, Mr. James Callaghan, M.P. for Cardiff South East, Chancellor of the Exchequer, announced in the House of Commons that a New Mint would be built at Llantrisant on a 30-acre site. Sir Alexander Gibb and Partners were appointed consulting engineers and Sir Frederick Gibbard, Consulting Architect. The main building contract was given to R. M. Douglas Construction Limited.

On Monday, 7th August, 1967, Mr. J. H. James, Deputy Master and Comptroller of the Royal Mint cut the first turf at Llantrisant to mark the beginning of the construction of the new Royal Mint in South Wales. On 19th February, 1968, Mr. James Callaghan laid the foundation stone.

Her Majesty Queen Elizabeth performed the opening ceremony when she pressed a button which set in motion the machine turning out the first of the new decimal coins to be produced in the new building. When in full production, the Royal Mint will employ 1,700 men many of whom will be recruited locally. Several workers are already being trained at a special training school set up at Bridgend.

The manufacture of coins takes place in two main stages. First is the production of plain discs or "blanks". Second is the stamping of these blanks with the obverse and reverse designs. The stamping has to be preceded by processes in which the blanks are softened, washed and inspected for defects. New coins are to be issued. A new 20p coin will come into use from June 1982 and a sovereign size £1.00 coin will come into use in April 1983.

The present buildings are equipped with five main sorts of plant all of which are linked by a modern system of mechanical handling. When fully operational the factory should be capable of producing between 50 and 60 million coins per week.

Already the New Mint has been christened 'The Welsh Fort Knox'. When the Mint moved to Llantrisant from Tower Hill, London, a thousand years of history changed direction.

The geographical position of Llantrisant may well help to preserve its character when the new town, now being built, will be surrounding the old town. In 1964, Glamorgan County Council in a publication entitled 'Glamorgan—A Planning Study', recommended the establishment of a new town at Llantrisant which would accommodate a population of over 100.000.

In order that Llantrisant might retain its identity and character, the County Planning Committee resolved that Mr. Gordon Cullen be engaged as Townscape Consultant to prepare a report. This report entitled, 'Llantrisant, A Welsh Hill Town' was published on 28th June, 1968.

The recommendations in the report outline a bright future for the old town and suggest good ideas for enhancing its natural character. Should the recommendations be implemented, Llantrisant will become a local centre for leisure activities. Mr. Cullen hores Llantrisant would have an inspirational function and become part of a whole network of views, open spaces, footpaths and woodlands which would interpenetrate the New Town. A further report was published by Dr. Buchanan who made a survey of the Cardiff area and this will have an effect on the overall development of this district.

On 1st April, 1969, the long-awaited report of Dr. Colin Buchanan was made public. The report recommended that Llantrisant be a new town. A town for the car-user and the age of affluence. The new town centre near Miskin will straddle the M4. The £381m new town will cover 10,000 acres which is almost the size of Cardiff, and will be south of the old town of Llantrisant. Development is to be phased over thirty years starting in 1971. It is estimated that the present population of 12,000 will rise to 94,000 in 1991 and 130,000 or 145,000 in 2001.

Today the Parish of Llantrisant has three churches within its boundary:—

The Parish Church dedicated to St. Illtyd, St. Gwynno, St. Tyfodwg (1400 *years old*).

Miskin Church dedicated to St. David (1907).

Beddau Church dedicated to St. Michael and All Angels (1936).

The Parish can be divided into three distinct parts, which show a development of three kinds of society:—

1. *The town of Llantrisant—walled and fortified through the ages with its special privileges granted by Charter.*
2. *Miskin Village—which shows the village structure of society —the Church, Manor and Inn.*
3. *Rural district of Beddau—once an area of prosperous farms and gentlemen's country residences—now a large modern industrial village which has grown from a group of houses at a cross-roads, within a hundred years.*

Llantrisant, steeped in tradition, is today the centre of a prosperous industrial district. The number of coal and iron works has noticeably decreased, but now there is a great variety of light industry. Housing projects are in active expansion and preparation in the surrounding districts. Although the face of Llantrisant is noticeably changing in appearance, several of the streets are still cobbled and steep. Many old cottages have been demolished and modern houses partly surround the Parish Church, but the Parish Offices, the Castle ruins, the Southgate toll-cottage and the Town Hall are reminders of the past when Llantrisant was a busy centre of trade and all who travel the district can admire the reassuring view of the "city that is set on an hill".

Pontyclun Carnival Parade, 1909

Pontyclun Coronation Procession, June 1911

St. Paul's Church, Pontyclun, b. 1895

Maes yr Felin Bridge, Pontyclun

The Old Flannel Mill, Rhiwsaeson in 1914
Kept by a Mr. Evans. The Mill is demolished

Thatched Cottage in Rhiwsaeson in 1906. This house now has a slate roof

Two views showing Film Unit shooting on location, at Llantrisant, the popular film of 1939 " Proud Valley " which starred Paul Robeson the renown bass singer

Tonysguboriau (Talbot Green) 1910

On the River Ely one mile from Llantrisant, by William Payne, circa 1800
(National Library of Wales)

Lanelay Hall and Drive at the beginning of the Century

Talbot Road, 1895

Llantrisant Road, Pontyclun

Cowbridge Road, Pontyclun, early 1900's

Footbridge
Llantrisant Station, Pontyclun in its heyday

Pontyclun Carnival Day, 1908

The Weir, Pontyclun

The Royal Mint, Llantrisant.
Model showing site of Royal Mint when all phases of building are completed

"GOREU ARF A DARF DERF[illegible] WR FO DOETH YW ARF DYSG."

Llantrisant School Board.

That Priscilla Williams

Was Examined by Her Majesty's Inspector

and passed in the various subjects of the 4th

Standard on June 6th 1887

Signed M John (Mistress)

"KNOWLEDGE IS POWER."

"GWELL DYSG NA GOLUD."

A Pupil's Certificate of 1887, Queen Victoria's Jubilee Year.
This belonged to the Author's Grandmother

Rose Hill, Llantrisant in 1910

Heol Sarn, Llantrisant, 1910

A view of Cross Inn in 1910

A view of Cross Inn in 1914

Delivering Coal at Southgate, Llantrisant, 1920's

A view of Rhiwsaeson in 1905

Two views of Brynsadler, 1910

The Old Church, Talygarn, now a ruin

St. Anne's Church, Talygarn

15. Talbot Green

Talbot Green lies to the south of Llantrisant town and has attained its present importance as a business centre because of its position at a cross-roads and as a junction for bus services. The original name of this village was Ton Ysguboriau (Barns in an Unploughed Field) which is the name now given to the school opened in the early years of this century. The community grew up at the cross-roads near the school in the 1860's. The Inn named the Talbot Arms commemorates the connection of this district with the Talbot family of Hensol Castle. The road leading to Llantrisant on which the now disused Salem Chapel (Bible Christians) is sited, was known as Talbot Road. The present Post Office and store was in existence in 1871 conducting business as a grocers and drapers under the name of Z. A. Cook. During World War II the shop was damaged in an air-raid but now the premises has been rebuilt and D. J. Lee & Co. is another long established business.

The most historic house is Lanelay House which was the home of the Bassett family who were descendants of Sir Philip Bassett, Lord of St. Hilary, whose family motto was "Gwell Angau na Chywilydd" (Better Death than Shame). The library once possessed some valuable documents, books and manuscripts. In 1866, the house was the property of N. E. Vaughan, Esq. In 1884 Sir Joseph Layton Elmes Spearman Bart, J.P. lived here and later the home of a Major Lee, M.P. and A. Vaughan Lee, Esq. During the 1890's the house was occupied by T. J. Masters, Esq., coal speculator and later founder of the well-known firm of clothiers. Colonel Bruce then took up residence and continued to live there for some years after World War I (1914-18). The house was then the home of Edmund Hann, Esq., who was employed by the Powell Duffryn Company. Since 1951, the house has been the headquarters of the Mid-Glamorgan Fire Service.

During the 1890's there was rapid development in the district and on 3rd September, 1909 a school was opened with David Llewellyn, Esq., the first headmaster. The present headmaster is Gwilym Moses, Esq. Talbot Green was just a small hamlet but with an early interest in sport. On the site of Llantrisant Motors opposite the Talbot Arms, there was a Quoit Ground and a race-course was established for many years where Y Pant Secondary School is now sited. During the twenties the Talbot Athletic Club flourished as did a gymnasium supervised by Geoffrey Retter, Esq., who was well-known for his feats of strength and reputed to be one of the strongest men able to hammer a six-inch nail into wood with his fist. He was a baker by trade and still lives at Talbot Green. Sport continues to flourish throughout the district. There is a flourishing Rifle Club here. The Coach, Glyn Williams,

Esq., was chosen as a member of the British Olympic team, to compete in Mexico during 1968.

Most of the social life was centred on Llantrisant but travelling shows have always been attracted here. Among the first were Wadbrook's Shows, Freeman's, John Studt's Switchback and Hippodrome Shows and Alexandra's Circus. These shows were eagerly awaited and well-patronised. At first the shows were set up in a field where Tonysguboriau School is now. In more recent times, fairs and circuses have been located on the Ely road near the Bus Station. In 1965, this site was developed into the Maes y Rhedyn Housing Estate. In addition to the several visiting shows there were visits to Garth Maelwg for picnics and to see the sulphur springs there provided pleasure. The mountain slopes of Garth Maelwg had been planted with larch, pine and spruce trees by the then Marquis of Bute in 1886, but most of this forest disappeared by 1916. For about ten years vegetation was allowed to grow unhindered. For just over fifty years the mountain slopes have been planted and supervised by the Forestry Commission. A magnificent view can be seen from several points in the parish of what is Wales' oldest state forest. The farm of this village was New Park and for many years was the home of the Joshua family. Members of this family are scattered throughout South Wales. Lyn Joshua is well-known as the lyric writer of the song " We'll keep a Welcome ". Another well-known member of the family is Rev. Seth Joshua, the evangelist.

New Park has now been re-developed. The Tesco Supermarket was opened in November 1979 and has dominated the site as a commercial centre. In September 1981, Leo's Home Centre was opened.

After the end of World War I the district had a further period when rapid development in housing and business interests took place. One of the chief reasons was that in 1921, the Government empowered local councils to provide houses in their various localities. This, together with further coal speculation at Ynysmaerdy and other works, made it necessary to have some form of road transport. At first there were many operators including Gough's, Mountain Ash and other speculators formed the Amalgamated Bus Services in 1927 operating the Beddau-Pontypridd route.

In 1922-3 the road from Talbot Green to Tonyrefail was laid and the " Rhondda Tramways Co. Ltd." started services from here to Cardiff via Tonyrefail and also there was a Beddau—Barry Island service organised by the " South Wales Commercial Motors ". These two companies have organised one of the most efficient bus services which exists in rural areas. The Western Welsh Omnibus Co. Ltd., came into existence in 1929 when the South Wales Commercial Motors (founded 1919) amalgamated with the passenger road services of Great Western Railway. The Rhondda Transport Company Ltd., started life as the " Rhondda Tramways Co. Ltd.", on 13th April, 1906 but changed to the present name in 1934. The Company's Diamond Jubilee occurred on 13th April, 1966.

The Rhondda Transport Company has now amalgamated with the Western Welsh Omnibus Company which since 1972 is now part of the National Bus Company.

Apart from the two major companies, bus services are provided by a private operator, W. A. & R. Edwards of Talbot Green. Mr. Edwards was one of the first to provide transport here in 1925. He started by conveying workers to the iron ore mines at Llanharry and over the years has provided valuable service conveying schoolchildren to schools and those workers requiring transport to places not on the regular bus routes.

The bus station was established on the present site in 1939. It is interesting to remember that Frank Reed, Esq., an inspector with the Rhondda Omnibus Co. Ltd., at Talbot Green, was instrumental in establishing Talbot Green as the name of the centre.

With improved transport facilities, people moved more easily from different parts of the district. Business expanded and the Penygraig Co-operative Society built and opened a store at Talbot Green, which replaced an eariler establishment at Commercial Street, Llantrisant, now Castle Stores. The new premises at Talbot Green, opened in 1932, became a show place in South Wales. When the Co-operative Congress met at Cardiff in 1935, delegates from all parts of Britain came to see this model shopping centre. They expressed admiration of the spacious grocery and provision store; the butchery department so well set back away from the dust and petrol fumes, and protected from the sun's rays by projecting walls; and the well-stocked dry-goods sections where a member could buy enough clothes and furnishings to stock a household. These premises were closed in September 1981 and business transferred to Leo's Home Centre. Near this store in 1934 Llantrisant Motors established their original garage, which was started by John Williams.

Just as the village was beginning to develop into an important centre the Second World War delayed plans. Since 1950, the village has doubled in size, due to the establishing of several housing estates. The first were Heol Johnson and Heol Miles (named after Alderman Johnson Miles, Cowbridge), and Fan Heulog and more recently Bron Haul. Private estates extend along the Ely Road and the grounds of Danygraig House now form a modern residential estate. Further development has taken place at Maes-y-Rhedyn and at Forest Hill on the Lanelay Road. The Golf Club was originally established in 1925. Meetings were held on Llantrisant Common. For about 50 years the Club has occupied its present clubhouse at Talbot Green where there is a good 9-hole course. It is also the site of the barn which gives Talbot Green its original name of Tonysguboriau (Barns in an unploughed field).

This increase in housing and population has encouraged many business premises to open at Talbot Green, making it an excellent shopping centre. In 1955, Danygraig House was taken over by the

Llantrisant and Llantwit Fardre Rural District Council. The house was originally built as a residence for Dr. Norton Davies. He maintained a priest to conduct Roman Catholic services for his family. The room which was used as the Council Chamber was formerly in use as a Roman Catholic Chapel. Roman Catholics now hold services at Penygawsi. The offices of the National Insurance are now at the Council's former address at School Street, Pontyclun.

In November, 1956, the Law Courts, which had formerly been held at the Town Hall, Llantrisant, moved to new premises at Talbot Green. Also in 1956 a new secondary school was opened called " Y Pant ". The first Headmaster was Mr. Brian Hill, B.A., who retired in August 1981. The present Headmaster is Mr. Peter Davies. The school has the motto " Byw trwy Ddysgu " (Live through Learning). The only place of worship is Ebenezer Free Church, which was built and supervised by E. J. Dickenson, Esq. Near the Law Courts stands a new school for spastic children. The Headmistress is Miss Garland. The School was opened in September, 1964. Talbot Green has developed as a new business centre and a new road from Cardiff to the Rhondda was brought into use in February, 1968. The new Ely Valley Telephone Exchange is centred here.

The Ely Valley Industrial Estate was started in 1967. Since the Royal Mint opened in December, 1968, other firms like Fram Filters, Perkin, Elmer and Powell Duffryn Engineering have established themselves. Considerable industrial development is being planned by Ronald Lyon (Estates) Co. Ltd.

Near the bus station a row of cottages stood which were once the homes of agricultural workers on the farm. The houses were demolished in 1969 and the new shopping precinct built. A new hostelry, " The Hand in Squirrel " opened in September, 1970. What was once the farmhouse is now Eden's business premises. Previously Mr. J. Lobb and his father conducted a long-established business as greengrocer here. In 1974, a familiar building was demolished, Morgan's Hairdressing Saloon which was built just prior to World War II. Here many an interesting discussion took place—a happy meeting place indeed.

Near Lanelay Hall, an industrial estate is expanding rapidly. The establishments of Ace Holdings, George Engineering and Budgen, formerly Batemans the Welsh Grocer, has been joined by L'Oreal, one of the world's leading manufacturers of hair toiletries and cosmetics. The firm is established in over 100 countries and possesses its own manufacturing factories in more than twenty countries. The United Kingdom factory is now housed in an ultra-modern production and administration complex here at Llantrisant. Initially the factory provides employment for more than 600 people.

16. Pontyclun

Pontyclun is a large village which has grown around a railway station named Llantrisant. The name Pontyclun is taken from a farmhouse situated near the confluence of the river Clun with the river Ely. Leland, who was Henry VIII's antiquarian, travelled Britain during the years 1538-1540 and recorded his description of this district: —

> " *There are two parkes by south of Llantrisant now paled and without deere. There is now Yrun made in one of the parkes named Glunog. The river Clunn or Clonne, now called Cloun, run through these lands, formerly parkes, and at the confluence of the river Clun with the Ely, a farm house still exists called Pontclun, or Pontcloun.*"

He also refers to a " Bridge of Pont Cloun of Wood ".

In several old documents and records Pontyclun is spelt as " Clunn " or " Cloone " and described as the Manor of Clun. From earliest times it has been in the hands of the chief Lords. Rice Merrick in his " Book of Glamorganshire Antiquities (1578) says: —

> " *Clunn, Lord of the Manour and Parke of Clunn, of his name soe called. In the Parke of Clunn remayneth the rubbish of his house called Bayly Clunn. The mannour in the Welsh tongue, is until this day called Trewerne.*"

An explanation of the name is: " Clun "—Clin—old Welsh word for meadow. Pontyclun means " the Meadow Bridge ". Wern or Gwern—name used for a swamp meadow. The " Park of Cloone " was the scene of capture of some of the party of soldiers who had accompanied Edward II when he was made prisoner in 1326 at Llantrisant Castle.

A survey of the Manor of Clunn dated 3rd December, 1666 states: " To the Articles 8, the said Jurors do present, and say there are mines of iron in the lower park of Clunn, and they say and present, that to their knowledge there are several mines or minerals of lead now or lately upon the Lord's demesne lands, within the Manor called Park Issa or Lower Park ".

Coal, iron, lead and limestone have been found in abundance in the district and the working of these raw materials has attracted trade and brought important development to the area around Llantrisant. The South Wales Railway reached as far as Llantrisant but further developments were planned.

During the sixties the Taff Vale Railway decided to develop communication between the Rhondda Valley and the Bristol Channel with the object of serving industrial development in this hilly district. The chief contractor was John Calvert. The Ely Valley Railway has been incorporated in 1857 and had opened a railroad from the South Wales

Railway at Llantrisant towards the Rhondda. This railway was opened in August 1860 to Tonyrefail and in 1862 extended to Penygraig. In 1861 the Great Western Railway had leased this railroad because they had acquired one of the Ely Valley Collieries for the purposes of Locomotive coal supply.

The Taff Vale backed the Llantrisant & Taff Vale Junction Railway which was incorporated in June 1861. The purpose of this Company was to develop the old Llantwit Fardre tramroad and to build a connection from the main line of the Taff Vale near Treforest to a junction with the Ely Valley at Maesaraul, 1½ miles north of Llantrisant. Running powers were granted over the Ely Valley from the junction into Llantrisant. The line was opened for freight traffic in December, 1863. Passenger service between Pontypridd and Llantrisant began on 21st January, 1875. This service continued until, for economic reasons, it was withdrawn on 31st March, 1952. The service to Penygraig was also discontinued. Many of the stations are now demolished and in 1965 the railway tracks dismantled. In 1969 the Treferig Valley Railway which was opened for goods traffic in April 1883 was closed in 1924 and the tracks dismantled in 1934.

The Cowbridge Railway was incorporated on 29th July, 1862 and opened in February 1865 from the G.W.R. station at Llantrisant to Cowbridge for goods and from September 1865 for passengers. When this line was extended and opened for traffic on 1st October, 1892, the original passenger terminus at Cowbridge became a goods depot and was replaced by a new station. The engine sheds at Cowbridge were closed in 1924. Passenger service below Cowbridge was withdrawn on 5th May, 1930 and freight traffic on 1st November, 1932. The track was dismantled in 1947. The passenger service from Llantrisant to Cowbridge was withdrawn on 26th November, 1951. This route was the first to have a diesel-car service.

Since 1951 there has been a decrease in the train services due to economic factors. There has been a marked change in the travelling habits of people in the whole of Britain, so much so that the Government instituted an enquiry into the working of the railways supervised by the redoubtable Dr. Beeching. One of the results of this action was the closing of Llantrisant Station in September, 1964. The main line trains from Cardiff now make their first stop at Bridgend. Now only memories of days gone by, when crowds of people came from the Rhondda to Llantrisant Station bound for Maesyfelin Farm fields where a day of games and picnics had been arranged, are left. This was a favourite Sunday School treat. During two World Wars the station helped in the war effort. During the period 1914-18, trains bringing coal from the Naval Colliery, Penygraig on its way to Portsmouth and Southampton were manned by Pontyclun crews. The cargo was popularly known as " Jellicoe's Coal ". These were the days when ships were using coal for power. While the crowds waited for returning trains, they passed the time with a spontaneous concert given on the platform. At this period there was a restaurant in the building, now occupied by the Pontyclun Social Clubs.

During World War II, Llantrisant was a busy centre for many trains each day conveyed hundreds of munition workers to factories at Bridgend, Cardiff and Treforest. A station on the main London—Swansea—Fishguard line and centred in an industrially prosperous and expanding industrial district could be most useful. During November and December 1965, all station buildings and platforms were demolished, except the main booking office which was also demolished in 1967.

Modern Pontyclun originated near the Llantrisant Railway Station. This consisted of School Street, Ely Street and part of Llantrisant Road between the School Street entrance and Bethel Baptist Chapel. The Windsor Arms (also a posting house) and Bute Hotel were in existence in 1871 and by 1878 the old National School in School Street was opened, it is now used by an engineering firm. The school was the centre of all social life in the early days and the Church of England services were held here under the direction of the Vicar of Llantrisant, who was responsible for this village right up to 1924. Population increased and an iron school was built in 1913-14, near the site of the present school. The school which is used now was opened in 1923. The school has the motto "Dring yn uchel Dring yn Uwch". (Climb high, climb higher). The present headmaster is Howard Thomas, Esq.

In September 1973 Maesyfelin Infants School was opened. This school is built on the open-plan principle. The first Headmistress was Miss Felicia Thomas, J.P. who retired in 1979. The present Headmistress is Mrs. Jean Jones.

Pontyclun was the chief rail centre and several industries in addition to iron and coal mines were started. In the 1870's the Llantrisant Gas Works was opened and supplied gas over an area of seven miles radius. No street lighting was supplied. This was an amenity which was provided after the new Llantrisant Rural District Council was established in 1894. Electrical street lighting appeared in 1925. This system was replaced in 1963-66 with modern fluorescent lighting at the cost of £130,000, and has been installed throughout the Llantrisant area.

Probably the oldest firm still operating at Pontyclun is the Ely Steam Joinery, founded in the 1870's. This firm still conducts business under the name of Pontyclun Electrical Joinery/Timber Works Ltd. The Ely Tin Plate Works, which also started in 1872, and situated near the railway line, was owned by a W. H. Edwards, Esq. The works consisted of four mills, a tin house and a finishing department. During the depression in the 1930's the works closed down (1934) and during World War II was a W.D. Stores. The site has been occupied since 1960 by a firm named Capener Caravan Window Makers. This firm was established in 1950 at Treforest.

Nearby, at the former Mountford Phillips Foundry is an American-owned firm, Kirk & Co. (Tubes) Ltd., who, with their subsidiary Cambrian Forge Foundry Ltd., have, since February 1965, been owned by the Chemerton Corporation of America. The factory at Pontyclun comprises a stamping shop, machine shop and a pipe work section. The firm which now owns this works, first introduced a process of forging seamless welding pipe fittings to America in 1927. The headquarters are located in Louisville, Kentucky. Now this site, which was first established in the 1890's as a colliery tram works of Messrs. David & Co., and as a munitions factory during World War I, has a bright future under new management. Nearby is the firm Bronze Smelters Ltd. This flourishing firm was started about 40 years ago by Mr. Thomas Jones.

Near Kirk & Co. (Tubes) Ltd., was located a Pipe and Sanitary Works which began as Messrs. Noel Ltd., and was one of the largest works of its kind with a world wide export business. This is now closed. These established industries have, since the end of World War II, been joined by several light industries : The Royal Sovereign Pencil Co. (1947) which has its principal centre here, Permutit Ltd., who make water softening apparatus, and E. M. Manufacturing Ltd., who make cosmetics, are all located at Loftus Terrace. The houses in Loftus Terrace were formerly owned by the now disused Coedcae Colliery Company and demolished in 1967. Now Tudor Jenkins, Yemm Holdings Ltd. and Pontyclun Service Station occupy the site. Leekes have an important centre here. Clean Plastics Ltd. occupy the old Parish Offices in Ely Street. Also in Ely Street is the Burridge Construction Company who have taken over the premises of Thomas Morgan, Wine and Beer Merchants. The firm of Thomas Morgan was long established here and was responsible for bringing the first steam waggon to be seen in South Wales. This was driven from the Thorneycroft Works in London to Pontyclun by William Long, Esq., in 1905. It was an attraction of the Bath and West Show which was held in Swansea the same year. Thomas Morgan moved to Bridgend soon after the end of World War II where the business is still flourishing. The premises is now used by Burridge Construction Co. Ltd., a civil enginering firm who came here in 1964. Also in Ely Street is the Fire Station which was built in 1925. A new Fire Station was built in 1978.

Pontyclun's expansion can be traced by following the development of its several non-conformist chapels. Each one is situated in a distinctive residential section. The earliest chapel is Bethel Baptist Chapel at Llantrisant Road, which was founded in 1876 and built in 1884. Others established were:—

Tabernacle, Independent, 1892.

Methodist Church, Cowbridge Road, 1899.

Hope Presbyterian Church, Cerdin Avenue, 1910

St. Paul's was built in 1895 after many years of work at the National School, Llantrisant Station. The contract was given to a local builder named John Morgan. The foundation stone was laid by Miss Masters of Lanelay on Wednesday, 15th August, 1894 at 3.30 p.m. A short service was performed in the Schoolroom, Llantrisant Station where a procession formed to march to the building site which adjoined the old Turnpike Gate. The church, which cost £1,600 to build was opened and licensed for Divine Worship by the Lord Bishop of Llandaff on Thursday, 27th June, 1895. Three services were held during the day when sermons were preached by the Bishop, the Rev. T. J. Bowen, Rector of Llangattock and the Rev. W. R. Thomas, M.A., Vicar of Abersychan. The Bishop's text " willeth all men to be saved, and to come unto the knowledge of the truth (I Tim. ii.4).

The Church, erected from plans of E. Bruce Vaughan, Esq., consists of chancel and nave. There is a peal of two bells in the bell-turret. The first curate in the new church was Rev. J. Williams who had only recently assisted at the service of the cremation of Dr. Price of Llantrisant. The church was under the jurisdiction of the Rev. Joshua Pritchard Hughes, Vicar of Llantrisant. When the Welsh Church was Disestablished in 1920, Pontyclun became a Parish in its own right in 1924. It is now described as the Parish of St. Paul's, Pontyclun with Talygarn. The first vicar of Pontyclun was Rev. John Jones-Davies who remained as vicar until his death in October, 1961. Rev. Roy Meredith Owen was inducted in June, 1962. The church has been renovated and a new organ installed, the organ has a detached console made by R. V. Gill of Cardiff Organ Works. The original organ was built by W. R. Richardson & Sons, Manchester and was presented by the Masters family of Lanelay Hall and dedicated on 21st May, 1897. The instrument has now been renovated and is used at St. Ann's Church, Talygarn.

On Sunday, 20th October, 1963, the Right Reverend T. M. Hughes, Assistant Bishop of Llandaff, consecrated an altar table and dedicated a reredos in memory of the first vicar, Rev. John Jones-Davies (1924-1961).

The oak altar table was the gift of the Misses Gertrude and Nancy Davies, sisters of the late vicar.

The altar stone is a marble slab, 15 ins. by 12 ins. and is incised with fine crosses (one at each corner and one in the centre) representing the Five Wounds of our Lord on the Cross. In the centre panel is the motif: I.H.S.—Iesus Hominum Salvator—Jesus the Saviour of Men.

The altar was made by Vanpoulles Ltd., of London.

The reredos is the gift of parishioners and friends of the late vicar. It was designed by Colin Shewring and made by the Warham Guild Ltd., of London. The description in the official programme is as follows:—

> " *It is a visual reminder of the two central teachings of the Christian religion that Christ suffered and died on the Cross, and the third day rose again from the dead. The Central Panel depicts the Easter Morning scene as recorded by Saint John*:—
>
> " *The first day of the week cometh Mary Magdalene early, when it was yet dark, unto the sepulchre, and seeth the stone taken away. Then she runneth and cometh unto Simon Peter and to the other disciple whom Jesus loved, and saith unto them, They have taken away the Lord out of the sepulchre, and we know not where they have laid him. ' Peter therefore went forth, and*

that other disciple and came to the sepulchre, . . . and saw the linen cloths lie and the napkin that was about his head, not lying with the linen cloths, but wrapped together in a place by itself . . . and saw and believed.' For as yet they knew not the scripture that he must rise from the dead.

"*But Mary stood without the sepulchre weeping, and as she wept, she stooped down and looked into the sepulchre, and seeth two angels sitting, the one at the head, and the other at the feet where the body of Jesus had lain . . .*"

The side panels show some of the instruments of our Lord's Passion:—

On the left, the hammer nails and spear with the drops of blood; on the right, the whips used in the scourging before crucifixion. The drops of blood are also seen in this panel.

"*He suffered under Pontius Pilate, Was crucified, dead and buried . . . And the third day He rose again from the dead . . .*"—Apostles' Creed.

The Memorial Table is inscribed:—

"*The Altar is the gift of Gertrude and Nancy Davies and is dedicated to the Glory of God, and in affectionate remembrance of their brother*:

John Jones-Davies, Priest,

FIRST VICAR OF THIS PARISH 1924-1961

The Reredos is the gift of his parishioners

"*I know that my Redeemer liveth.*"

On 7th November, 1965 a new stained-glass window was unveiled in memory of George R. A. Wilson, Lay Reader of the Parish of Pontyclun and Headmaster of Pendoylan Church School.

Description:—

This new stained glass window is in the north wall of the Church, immediately facing the door. Its striking design of luminous pale golds contrasting with a harmony of rich blues and purples, catches the eyes of all who enter the Church. It demonstrates that a true work of art for the Church can be an act of worship in itself. It is a visual 'Venite' saying 'O Come, let us sing unto the Lord, let us heartily rejoice in the strength of our salvation'.

The subject of the window—appropriate to the nature of stained glass—is Light itself: "A Light shineth in Darkness". A central orb of light sings at the head of the window and sweeps across and down the apertures, dominating the network of dark thorn shapes at the base, and so expressing the victory of light over darkness—the light of God's Work and Promise conquering evil and ignorance and the entangling complexities of life on earth. Through the web of thorns are seen the words 'THY LIGHT BREAK FORTH . . .'

This subject was chosen for its link with the vocation of the man whose memory the window now perpetuates—his services to the Church as a Lay Reader, and to the community as a School Teacher. The inscription at the foot of the window reads:—

IN MEMORY OF GEORGE R. A. WILSON,
LAY READER OF THIS PARISH, 9 Jan. 1962.
R.I.P.

The window has been designed by John Petts at his studio-workshop at Llanstephen, Carmarthen. Mr. Petts also made the Alabama Window, given by the people of Wales through the "Western Mail" to the Baptist Church, Alabama, U.S.A.

The window has been given by Mr. Cyril Brown, J.P., Bron-y-gocyd, Llanilterne.

A new church hall was dedicated by Bishop T. M. Hughes on Palm Sunday, 1969, and a modern vicarage blessed by Dr. Glyn Simon, Archbishop of Wales, on 31st August, 1969. The present Vicar is Rev. David John, B.A.

Pontyclun continued to be a flourishing business centre and in 1910, Godfrey L. Clarke, Esq., of Talygarn House, built the Institute at Pontyclun for the use of the inhabitants of Brynsadler and Pontyclun. The building was equipped for games and was a much needed place for leisure pursuits. In the original deeds it was stated that "No liquor, religious or political meetings" could be allowed there. The Institute was supervised by Trustees set up by Godfrey Clark himself. There was also a committee. Those who made use of the facilities were required to pay a monthly subscription of one shilling. The Bowls Club, founded in 1932, is still flourishing. During World War I the building was used as a hospital for wounded soldiers. A plaque in the main entrance is a reminder of the time:—

Pontyclun Institute
used as Red Cross Auxiliary Hospital
March 1915—*February* 1919
661 *patients treated.*

Commandants
Dr Logie March 1915—*July* 1915.
Mrs. O'Rorke August 1915—*February* 1919.

Medical Officers
Dr. Logie   *Dr. Tucker.*

Commandants of Detachments

Pontyclun	Llantwit	Llanharan
Dr. Logie	*Mrs. Bruce*	*Mrs. Tucker*
	Mrs. O'Rorke	

During this time one of the great singing stars of the day, Miss Sybil Vane, visited Pontyclun and entertained the patients here.

On the fire-place is inscribed the date 1910 and the inscription " In quo corriget? " (How may he improve himself?) During its existence the Institute has experienced good and bad times. Dances were held here during World War II and after. These proved very successful. By 1958 the established pattern of entertainment and leisure time had changed. It was necessary to change the Institute into a licensed club and it is now known as the Pontyclun Athletic Club. This is now the headquarters of all sporting organisations in Pontyclun. The Bowling Club continues but a car park now replaces the once much-used tennis courts. The club has a thousand members and there are plans for extending the building with additional facilities.

In the earlier years the social life comprised fund-raising teas and concerts at the National Schools together with visits to the many touring fairs, shows and circuses that came to the village. Some of the best known and remembered shows were those brought by John Studt. In 1912 the old show cinema established itself at Pontyclun near the Windsor Arms Hotel and was a source of entertainment until it closed on 8th March, 1932. This was replaced by the present cinema in Cowbridge Road which opened on 10th March, 1932. This cinema, together with other cinemas at Llanharan and Pencoed, formed the Studt circuit. The Pontyclun Cinema is now used for bingo sessions. The cinema was managed by Philip Phillips, Esq., grandson of John Studt who toured this district with his many and varied attractions.

It is interesting to remember that the Public Libraries Act was implemented in 1921 when the County Library was founded and established at the old school in Pontyclun. The first County Librarian who was to organise the system of lending books was Professor Saunders Lewis (b.1893), who is now nationally known as a distinguished novelist and playwright. In 1926, the Glamorgan County Council took over the Carnegie Library at Bridgend and the Library Headquarters has been established there ever since.

Pontyclun continued to grow in the 1930's and the erection of houses has continued on a large scale into the 1960's. Maesyfelin, once a farm of note in this district, has been developed into a modern housing estate.

Situated at the southern limits of Pontyclun is the War Memorial and recreation ground and nearby is the Masonic Temple.

The temple is the headquarters of the Trisant Lodge of the Grand Order of Free Masons. Although the Trisant Lodge was founded in 1920, the Pontyclun Temple was not built until 1929-30.

Over the bridge from Pontyclun is Brynsadler. The Ivor Arms was established in 1856 and opposite it stood the old Three Crowns Brewery. The old brewery existed until the early post-war years when it was replaced by the present United Clubs Brewery building. This has been set back from the road and has gardens in front of it. The hamlet of Brynsadler itself was formerly part of the Talygarn Estate, but the name always causes interest and discussion. Records show that in 1538, the Crown interest in the Park of Cloun and within three miles of it was subleased to John Sadler, an Alderman of the City of London. By 1540, Sadler rented to a William Kendall, a Cornish miner of Launceston who entirely reorganised the production of wrought iron from harder ores. By 1545 Kendall was in financial difficulties and sued by John Sadler. Kendall was imprisoned for non-payment of rent and later the works were acquired by John Sadler under new management and after whom Bryn Sadler is named. During 1974 the Nonconformist Church in the village was redesigned to become a beautiful modern residence.

17. Talygarn

Talygarn (Top of the cairn) lies in the Parish of Pontyclun, four miles from Cowbridge. Today it is an expanding residential community.

The church dedicated to St. Ann was once a chapelry of ancient foundation and under the jurisdiction of the Vicar of Llantrisant, but is now administered by the Vicar of Pontyclun. This ancient church was restored in 1687 by Sir Leoline Jenkins (1625-1685). He was born at Ty'r Ffald, near Talygarn. Leoline Jenkins was one of the early pioneers of Welsh Education. After attending Cowbridge Grammar School (founded 1608) he went to Jesus College Oxford (founded by Queen Elizabeth I in 1571 on the petition of Dr. Hugh Price of Brecon) in 1641. His studies however were interrupted by the outbreak of the Civil War in which he supported the Royalists. At the Restoration, Sir Leoline returned to Jesus College, was elected Fellow and in 1661, Principal of the College. His legal and diplomatic talents were in constant demand by the Government. Leoline Jenkins was knighted in 1670 and in 1680 he became a Privy Councillor and Secretary of State. He died in 1685.

His worthy, benevolent reputation lives on and is recorded in the private diaries of Samuel Pepys. He made many charitable endowments in the Vale of Glamorgan and was a benefactor of Cowbridge Grammar School.

In modern times Talygarn is well known as the residence of George T. Clark (1809-1898). This man, who achieved fame as an antiquarian and who was an authority on Glamorgan Mediaeval History, was an engineer by profession working on the Great Western Railway with Brunel. In 1846 he returned from doing Government work in India and married Ann Price in 1850. She was the daughter of Henry Lewis of Green Meadow, Tongwynlais. Henry Lewis' family had established the Dowlais Ironworks for the Guest family. Henry Lewis had also helped Sir Henry Bessemer in perfecting his process of steel manufacture. The widow of Henry Lewis eventually married Benjamin Disraeli, Lord Beaconsfield.

In 1887, George Clark rebuilt Talygarn Church in memory of his wife Ann. It is a stone building and consists of chancel, nave, south porch and a south tower. The floor of the tower is open to the nave. The church contains memorials to the Clark family. In the 1890's the living was held by Rev. Wm. Franklin Evans, M.A., Headmaster of Cowbridge Grammar School in the gift from Jesus College, Oxford. Recently new candlesticks and a font were dedicated in memory of the churchwarden and the interior has been redecorated.

George Clark took an active part in county affairs and made many valuable contributions to journals. He collected and published "The

Genaeologies of Morgan and Glamorgan (1886)" and "The Land of Morgan".

From 1898 until 1920, Talygarn was the home of Godfrey L. Clark, J.P., High Sheriff of Glamorgan. He is respected for the benevolent interest which he took in the affairs of the district. He was the first Chairman of the Llantrisant and Llantwit Fardre Rural District Council in 1894. By the direction of Wyndham Damer Clark, Esq., the Talygarn Estate was sold by auction on Tuesday, 4th July, 1922 at the Park Hotel, Cardiff.

The large mansion stands in beautiful ornamental gardens which has a lake, and a pathway made of champagne bottles which, when spent, were hammered into the ground, the bottle bottoms forming the surface of the path. The estate extended at 1,200 acres.

In the drawing room, billiards room, reception hall and main corridor are many fine examples by Biraghi, effected in 1895, the work for the most part by this well-known Italian artist being in the Venetian style, depicting various allegorical subjects, heraldic devices, Cupid and Caryatide figures, scrolls and arabesques featuring labour, art, etc. There are also some very massive and finely carved Carrara marble mantlepieces. The ceilings in the drawing room and reception hall are decorated with a large elliptical centre oil painting, surrounded by numerous other paintings of allegorical and mythological subjects. Electricity was installed in 1900 by the well-known engineering firm, Messrs. Drake and Gorham of London. There was also an internal telephone service. Since the auction of the estate in 1922, the house became a convalescent home administered by the South Wales Miners' Committee.

The new M4 motorway through South Wales will pass through the village.

18. Miskin Village

Miskin is a village situated two miles south of Llantrisant. It has grown up around the ancient Manor house which is now the home of Sir Brandon Rhys-Williams, Bart., M.P. for Kensington. The name of Miscin (Maes Cun—lovely plain) dates from early times and was the name given to one of the four Commotes in the Pennythen Cantref.

The system of dividing land into Commotes and Cantrefs was established in the Venedotion Code by Hywel Dda in the year 940. Miscin was a Cwmwd—house bearing the name of Miscin. During the period when the Normans were establishing themselves in Britain, Sir Robert Fitzhammon was created a Prince of Glamorgan by King William Rufus and was given lands for his services to the king. Fitzhammon established himself at Cardiff and divided his lands in Glamorgan between knights and their followers. There were 26 manors established altogether. These were all small in size. The Feudal land system superseded the old Welsh one of Commotes. The Lord of the Manor had certain privileges: " Jura Regalia ", felon's goods, flotsam and jetsam (right of wreck) and minerals under common lands. The tenants were " in capite "—bound to and in the defence of Cardiff if attacked.

The Norman plan was to dispossess the Welsh of the Bro (low) lands near the coast and drive the Welsh to the Blaenau (mountainous north where the ground was poor for cultivation). Hence the name Broviskin. The Broviskin and Bute Limestone Quarries at Mwyndy have been extensively worked. Mwyndy is reputed to have had iron works during the time of the Roman occupation of Britain. The Lord of Glamorgan during the conquest was Iestyn ab Gwrgan. In the year 1092 he gave his daughter in marriage to ap Einon ab Collwyn who occupied Miscin at this time. There were three sons and one daughter who occupied the Mansion. There is an effigy in Llantrisant Church of Cadwgan Fawr of Miscin who resided at the old manor. Near the old house was a monastery. It is reputed to have been dedicated to St. Cawrdav (Llancawrdav) and that the ruins of Miscin are all that are left of the Ancient Church of Cawrdav.

There is mention of Ivor Hir occupying the house. During his tour of this district about 1540, Leland mentions Cardiff having a " Miskin Gate ", and Miscin is known to have been a lordship during Tudor times. The seventeenth century saw the Herbert family resident there. They were Earls of Pembroke and Montgomery. The last lord was the Marquis of Bute who was also Lord of the Borough of Llantrisant. The manor has been occupied by several families among them the Bassett family who were respected for their benevolence. The family appears frequently in Llantrisant written documents. In Llantrisant church there is a brass chandelier inscribed " Gift of Mrs. Anne Bassett of Miskin to the Parish Church of Llantrisant ". The present Manor house at Miskin is built on part of the foundations of an older structure. An arch belonging to the former house is still visible from the courtyard. The property was purchased by David Williams Esq., during the mid-nineteenth century. The family was originally from Aberpergwm, Neath, but had come to live at Castellau Fawr in 1808.

David Williams was a well-known Welsh Bard with the Bardic title "Alaw Goch ". The establishment of the National Eisteddfod owes much to his generous, philanthropic disposition. Since the late nineteenth century the house was the home of David Williams' son, Judge Gwilym Williams. Gwilym Williams (1839-1906) received his early education from a tutor named Pethrick in Penrhiw Pennar Cottage, Cefn Pennar, Mountain Ash. The house, popularly known as Ty'r Pethrick, had some interesting architectural characteristics. Inside this small cottage was a wide staircase made of mahogany and oak. Over the library door was a painting which concealed a safe. It was in this room, lined with imitation bookshelves, that Gwilym Williams had received tuition. In the living room, the fireplace was situated under the window and the sill acted as the mantlepiece. The house eventually passed to Lord Aberdare and became the house of the groundsman of the local Golf Club. The house still exists today.

Miskin Manor house and grounds were developed until, by 1900, there was a most charming residence on a site which commands beautiful views of the surrounding countryside. The grounds and gardens with shrubs and tropical plants were considered to be the finest in the county. After a lapse of about 800 years there was a descendant of Iestyn ab Gwrgan who in turn was a descendant of Caractacus (Caradoc) who fought against the Romans and was taken to Rome in chains, living at Miskin Manor—namely Mrs. Gwilym Williams. Gwilym Williams was a magistrate of the county then. Stipendary Magistrate for this district (12 years) he was later appointed a County Court Judge for the Mid-Wales circuit and subsequently as County Court Judge for Brecon, Pontypridd, Merthyr, Aberdare, Bridgend and Swansea. He was also Admiralty Judge for the Port and Chairman of the Quarter Sessions. He died in 1906.

The exact date of the village of Miskin is not known, but Worrall's Directory for 1871 lists the following businesses as being in existence:—

Miskin Arms:	*Edmund Edwards, Esq.*
Blacksmith:	*William Charles, Esq.*
Mill:	*Mrs. Edward John*
Butcher:	*Morgan Thomas, Esq.*
Grocer:	*Daniel Morgan, Esq.* *Mary Thomas*
Joiner:	*Daniel Morgan, Esq.*
Boot and Shoe Makers:	*Thomas Thomas, Esq.* *Richard Bevan, Esq.*
New Mill School:	*Thomas Hughes, Master.*

Ebenezer, Welsh Methodist Chapel, founded in 1860, is still used for worship.

The Village School was built in 1875 but was closed in December 1962 because of the decrease in the number of children attending it. The building is now used by the Mid-Glamorgan County Playingfield Service, who store equipment there and the School house is used as administrative offices. Children from Miskin now attend Pontyclun Primary School. The last headmaster was Howard Thomas, Esq., who is the present headmaster of Pontyclun School.

In the nineteenth century Miskin was known as New Mill, after the Water Mill near the Manor which was still working during the early years of this century. Part of the building is still used as headquarters for the local Scout Troop. The land near the Mill was sold in 1959 and the funds used to make a silver loving cup. The cup is engraved with emblems depicting the story of the five loaves and two fishes, and the three saints, Illtud, Gwynno and Tyfodwg. At the bottom of the cup a Mill wheel is engraved. The cup was presented by Sir Brandon Rhys-Williams to his fellow Freemen of Llantrisant in 1960.

Although Miskin had an iron church, which had been built in 1878, it was felt that a more permanent building was needed. During the years 1900-7 people in the area were active in raising funds towards the cost of the building. The church was eventually opened in 1907 and is dedicated to St. David. This modern church is built in the decorated style and is cruciform in plan, with an embattled western tower. The stained-glass windows are unusual due to the fact that they bear many inscriptions in the Welsh language. In October, 1965, a new stained-glass window was unveiled in memory of Lady Juliet Rhys-Williams. The window was designed by Miss Jessie Bayes, who is an established artist in this type of work. She is one of the few people still alive who actually worked with the last of the Pre-Raphaelites and knew William Morris well. Miss Bayes is especially interested in the mystical side of Christianity and is influenced by the ideas of Eckhard. The new window is traditional in style and depicts Our Lord and a kneeling figure which represents " The Seeking Soul ". The inscribed text is: "Ask, and it shall be given you; seek, and ye shall find; knock and it shall be opened unto you." (St. Luke XI v.9), a favourite verse of Lady Rhys-Williams.

Miss Bayes also designed the windows dedicated to the memory of Sir Rhys-Williams and his eldest son, both of which are in Miskin Church.

Members of the Williams family are buried in the churchyard. In recent years the Manor was the home of Sir Rhys and Lady Juliet Rhys-Williams who were well-known for their public work. Lady Juliet Rhys-Williams, who died in September 1964, held important national appointments of a social nature. She served a term on the Board of Governors of the B.B.C. (1952-56) and Chairman of Cwmbran New Town Corporation. She was the author of several novels and books on taxation and economics. Her greatest work was in connection with

Child Welfare Maternity Services. Lady Juliet was the daughter of Clayton Louis Glyn and Elinor Glyn the romantic novelist. Elinor Glyn spent her last years at Miskin Manor and died there in 1937. During the second World War, the house was used as a convalescent home by the Red Cross and was visited at this time by Princess Marina, formerly Duchess of Kent. With her husband, Lady Rhys-Williams was responsible for founding a second church in the parish at Beddau in 1936. In this building is seen an ultra-modern design; it was dedicated to St. Michael and All Angels. The Manor itself has been twice ravaged by fire. Luxury flats now occupy most of the house but it is still used as a family home by Sir Brandon Rhys-Williams and his family.

Miskin has a long history and the village with its Church, Inn and cottages surrounding the War Memorial on the square has long been a familiar scene to many people in the district. Now, inevitably, during the second half of the twentieth century, progress has intruded and new private housing estates have been developed in the village.

19. Mwyndy

Near Miskin is Mwyndy (Tir Mwyn-dai)—Mellow House—which is a hamlet situated at a road junction on the Llantrisant—Cardiff Road and an old centre of industry. Evidence of an earlier settlement was unearthed here in 1762 when some Roman coins, cinders and earthenware were discovered. The Mwyndy Iron Works were started here in May, 1855, by R. Beaumont, Esq. The works were then owned by N. E. Vaughan, Esq. The last managers were William and Stephen Vivian in the 1870's-1880's. These works have been closed for many years. Mwyndy is now a centre of quarrying. The Broviskin and Bute Limestone Quarries, formerly owned in the 1890's by T. E. Williams, Esq., is now owned by Arthur Davies, Esq., and Idris Thomas who manufacture breeze blocks and are known as "Maxitet". Nearby is the Miskin Lime Company, which was started by Arthur Davies, Esq., and David Charles Israel, Esq., soon after World War II. The works operate at Pantyquesta Quarry and the kilns are situated at Mwyndy. Also nearby is the firm Mineral Supplies Ltd. Quarrying is still carried on at Hendy Quarry which was started by Evan Roberts, Esq., of Cardiff, the well-known firm of Clothiers in Queen Street. The business is now owned by English China Clay Ltd.

Mwyndy House, a gentleman's residence, is well-known for its well-kept gardens and its swimming pool. It was once the home of industrialists and more recently that of Col. R. Horley, Registrar to the Church in Wales in Llandaff Diocese. At the present time it is the home of Dr. Watkins and Dr. Eileen G. Watkins, Medical Officer of Health to the Llantrisant and Llantwit Fardre Rural District Council. The Llantrisant and District Motorcycle Club hold 'Motorcycle Scramble Competitions' here. These are popular and well patronised. Since the construction of the new road in 1968 the old village shop was rebuilt on its present site. The house is called "Haveachat". This is because the owner hopes that passers-by would come into the shop for social as well as commercial reasons. This continues the tradition of the village shop being an important social centre.

A mile down the road from Mwyndy is the hamlet of Croesfaen (Stone Cross) which has changed little in recent years except that a few new houses have been built. There is Saint David's Church near the Dynevor Arms Inn and a Non-Conformist Chapel, Babell (1866).

20. Hensol Castle

A short distance from Miskin Village is the large castellated mansion, Hensol Castle. The original building on this site was called by various names, viz.: " Hen Starle ", " Hen Ystafell " or " Hen Sail " which means " old foundation ". Place names surrounding the castle remind us of its importance as a fortified place. In the vicinity of the castle are farms called " Cefn Llys " (back of the court), " Caer Gwanaf (lesser forts) and a cottage called " Castell Bach " (small castle).

The house became the county seat of the Jenkins family in 1672 when land was leased by David Jenkins of Grays Inn, Middlesex, a Justice of the Western Circuit of Wales. The lease was made with William Morgan also of Grays Inn, Middlesex. David Jenkins was a supporter of Charles I during the Civil War. He is buried in Cowbridge Church. His son also named David Jenkins inherited the castle and after him his son Richard, who was well-known as a harpist and last of the Jenkins of Hensol, Cecil Jenkins, the grand-daughter of the Judge married Charles Mathew of Castell Mynach and their daughter married Charles Talbot.

Charles Talbot was a member of the Talbot family of Margam Abbey. Originally, the family came from Laycock Abbey, Wiltshire in the 17th century when John Ivory Talbot married Mary Mansel. He was related to Henry Fox Talbot (1800-1877) who invented the box camera, and gained renown as a noted early photographer. Charles Talbot was a lawyer and Solicitor General and then Lord Chancellor. He was raised to the Peerage with the title of Baron Hensol of Hensol. Later the title of Earl of Shrewsbury was added. During the residence of the Earl of Shrewsbury, the castle was styled in its present form, the work being completed in 1770. Earl Talbot died in 1782 and was succeeded by his son William. The castle passed into the ownership of the Barons Dynevor, whose descendants, the Wingfield family of Barrington Park, Oxfordshire, still own land in this district. At the close of the 18th century, the Talbot family left Hensol and the Castle was bought by Samuel Richardson from Gloucestershire who was a pioneer in agriculture. He carried out great improvements on land drainage and amongst other things he introduced the threshing machine to replace the old flail method of extracting seed from corn. The lakes at Hensol were constructed during his time here. Richardson sold the estate in 1840 to the Crawshays of Cyfarthfa.

During the period of Crawshay ownership the castle was the residence until 1823 of Benjamin Hall, son of Dr. Benjamin Hall, Chancellor of Llandaff and father of Sir Benjamin Hall who became Chief Commissioner for Works in 1855. During his period of office the clock tower of the Houses of Parliament was built and called " Big Ben " after Sir Benjamin Hall who was a tall figure of a man. In 1859 he was raised to the Peerage as Lord Llanover and two years later became Lord Lieutenant of Monmouthshire. Lady Llanover was a great patron of the Welsh Language and customs and a member of the Gorsedd of Bards. Altogether two celebrated ironmasters came to live at Hensol. William Crawshay was the first in 1829. Following the departure of the Crawshays, Hensol Castle was bought by one of another family of iron-masters, the Fothergills of Abernant, a Mr. Bertrand Fothergill. He died in 1871. The estate passed to his sister Miss Mary Fothergill who also died in 1871. Another sister, Mrs. Tarlton of Killeigh Abbey, Co. Offaly, Ireland, inherited the estate. She died in 1896 and the estate became the property of her daughter, Lady Isabella Elizabeth Price-Fothergill, and a niece of Rowland Fothergill, iron-master, who had died in 1869. Lady Fothergill married Sir Lambert Rose Price, Third Baronet and a Lieutenant in Her Majesty's 5th Lancers. Lady Fothergill died on the 30th November, 1918 and the estate was inherited by her only son, Sir Francis Rose Price, Bart., who left Hensol in 1926. In 1927 the Glamorgan County Council purchased the Hensol estate of 1,105 acres for £36,500. The house was to be used as a hospital.

New hospital blocks were built in 1935 and now most of the mansion is used for administration purposes. In 1948 the hospital was taken over by the Morgannwg Hospital Committee who have supervised the estate until 1st April 1974 when the Reorganisation of Local Government authority was vested in the Ogwr Community Health Council under the Mid-Glamorgan Area Health Authority. In December 1958, part of the estate was sold by order of the Ministry of Health. The Forestry Commission care for part of the estate but the hospital board still retain the farm and gardens near the mansion. Hensol Castle is now part of a hospital for nervous disorders for South, Mid and West Glamorgan, with other establishments at Parc, Glanrhyd and Penyfai in Bridgend.

Since leaving Hensol Castle, the son of Sir Francis Rose Price became internationally famous as an actor on stage, films, radio and television, known as Dennis Price. He was born in 1915 as Dennistoun Franklyn John Rose-Price, and became a frequent visitor to Hensol Castle. He made his stage debut in 1937 and his first film was released in 1944. Dennis Price was the British light leading man of his time and latterly equally light character actor. He can frequently be seen in his films on television but will be remembered for his part of Jeeves in the long-running T.V. series, " The World of Wooster ". He died in 1972 in the Channel Isles.

21. Beddau (Croes-y-Heol-y-Beddau)

Beddau is a new and rapidly expanding village situated two miles from Llantrisant. Beddau means graves and the place was known as Croesheol-y-beddau (Cross Road of the Graves). Two explanations are traditionally offered of the name Beddau; either, due to the importance of the district in time of tribal wars, Beddau is one of " divers places made notorious by their slaughter " or it is also known that felons were hanged from a tree at the cross roads and buried beneath the gallows.

In 1540 Leland who toured Britain mentions this district when describing the countryside around Llantrisant, he says: " There is now yrun made in one of the parkes named Glunog ". He was referring to hunting deer in the parklands here.

The district where Beddau now stands was predominantly a rural community with a farming economy. It is said that the dairy produce, etc., was exported to ports across the Bristol Channel. Most of the farms are nearly three hundred years old. The most important form in the village was Ty'n-y-nant farm situated near Nant Myddlyn. It is from this farm, on the Earl of Plymouth's estate, that Tynant has its name. Nearby stood Tynant Dingle (woodlands) where the Squire of Castellau would participate in fox hunting. The hunt was a famous one and there was a song about it called " The Hounds of Castellau ". Fox hunting was one of the chief pastimes and covered a wide area which included the boggy treacherous Gwaun Miskin, Ty Twarch and Tir-Mab-Ellis. There was also the attraction of the little inn at Castellau.

Ty'n-y-Nant farm was the oldest building in the village of Beddau. The Williams family have always farmed it during its four hundred years of existence. The family hold the record of being the oldest tenants in the whole of the Plymouth Estates. In 1948, the Earl of Plymouth sold the farm to its last inhabitant, Ivor Williams, Esq., and in 1952 the National Coal Board purchased the farmhouse and land, and today the farmhouse is purely a dwelling house. The land is used up by developments in the Cwm Colliery. Mrs. Williams left Tynant in 1966. The farmhouse became derelict and was demolished in 1969.

Ty'n-y-Nant farm reached its most flourishing period during the second half of the nineteenth century and early years of the twentieth. Ebenezer Williams had a reputation throughout the district of being an excellent farmer. Many people came to see his hay ricks which were considered works of art. The grain was ground at Castellau Mill and the milk sold wholesale. There was also a haulage business. Documents at the farm recorded that:—

" *Barley was carried from Coedcabach on Tynant farm on Friday, the 2nd day of November,* 1860."

" *and also wheat carried on Maesbach farm on Tuesday the 1st day of Janr.* 1861."

All traffic was horse-drawn and when the first train passed by, one of the horses going with milk to Treforest bolted with fright! The Woodlands had no proper road and was often a barrier to traffic. Very often carts would be stuck axle-deep in mud. Near the Woodlands is Croes-gêd House. It was the home of Squire Perkins and later of Samuel Evans, Esq., J.P., a magistrate formerly of Treferig Mansion. In addition to farming his own land, Ebenezer Williams was bailiff for the Hewett family at Tir-Mab-Ellis, and also a councillor. As a parish councillor, it was his responsibility to collect the rates and order materials for repairs to roads etc., and pay the workmen who did council jobs. During this period, a gamekeeper patrolled Gwaun Miskin.

On the edge of Gwaun Miskin stands Ty Twarch (Turf House). The original name was Cloddiau'r Cabin (Turf Cabin) and it is thought to date from early times when a custom was in vogue that a man had the right to land if he built a house of turf, and if the smoke went straight up through the chimney. Ty Twarch also flourished during the end of the nineteenth century and the owner at that time, Mary Thomas, had a retail milk round in Llantrisant.

The present owners took over the farm in 1915, and the second Ty Twarch house which stands alongside the original farmhouse was built by George Edwards, Esq., in 1915. Part of the farmyard was converted into garages for buses in 1923, but the rest of the land was cultivated until 1954, when the Rural District Council bought the land for building houses. Nearby Ty Twarch stands a new building which dominates the skyline. This is Gwaunrhydd, a block of flats for Senior Citizens who took up residence in July 1973.

Early in the nineteenth century, coal was mined at Dinas, in the Rhondda Valley. This marked the change from pasture to industry.

The first speculator to work coal on a large scale was Thomas Powell, Esq., whose attention was first attracted to the coal mines of Llantwit Fardre. He was very wealthy and successful. The coal pits of Dduhewid, Ystradberwig and Ty'n-y-Nant yielded 140,000 tons during the period they were working. The owner's son, also named Thomas Powell, was responsible for these pits and lived at Ida House, Tynant. He and his family were ambushed by natives in Abyssinia in April 1872. There have been many coal pits and levels in the area surrounding Beddau on the estates of Williams Aberpergwm and the Earl of Plymouth.

Many of the sources of coal were short lived. The Gelynog pit was open the longest. The original house is still standing near the workings and is known as Pooley's House. Near the house a railway crossed the roadway. Opposite Pooley's House stood another cottage called Gwerna which was in existence long before the Gelynog Colliery began operations. In the fields behind the school was a coal level and was known locally as " Strip and at it ". Other local names were " Dress and leave it ", " Snipe and Grouse " and near the Lamb and Flag, Castellau, was a level known as the " Bug and Flea ". The Ty'n-y-Nant (the Charles Pit) and Gelynog pits were very important. The best quality house coal was obtained there and was known as number three Llantwit red

Gelynog Inn — 1903

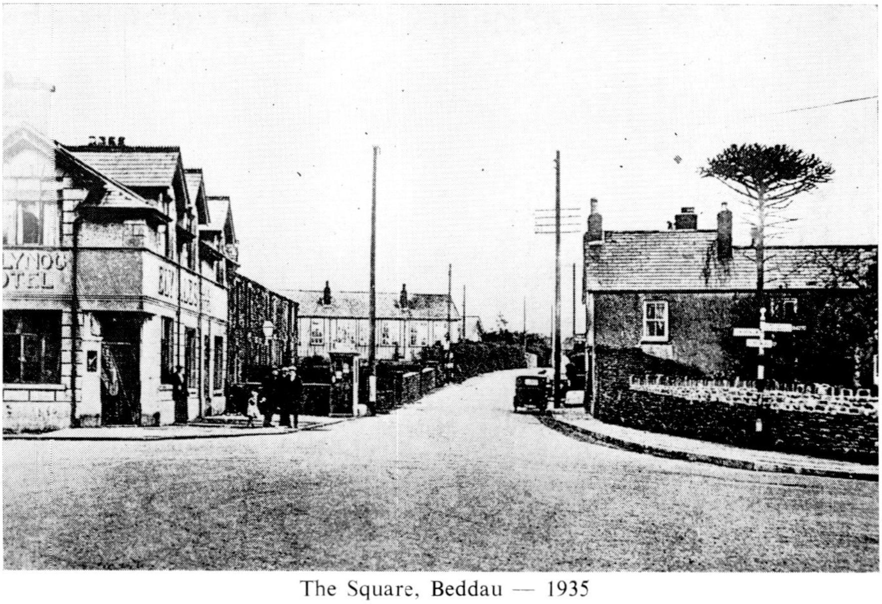

The Square, Beddau — 1935

Llantrisant Road — 1935

Parish Road, Tynant, 1935

First Sunday School, Zion Chapel, February 1920

Beddau — 1921
Drum Head Service conducted by Canon William Evans

The Welfare Hall — Laying the Foundation Stone, 1932

The Opening of the Welfare Hall, 1933

" Under the Palms " — Zion Chapel, 1924

"A Daughter of Moab " — Mount Pleasant Cantata

Two views of Cwm Colliery — 1912
(showing sinkers and workmen)

Bethania Chapel built 1867. Demolished 1974

Cwm Colliery — Wednesday, 13th October, 1909 — Cutting the First Turf

The Welfare Hall, Beddau

Aerial View of Cwm Colliery and Coking Plant
(Aero Pictorial Limited)

ash. The coal was expensive. Coal could be obtained at this period for three shillings and ten shillings a cart load. The cheaper coal coming from the levels. There was a hauliers' strike in 1893. By 1866, searching for coal extended to the Llantrisant Common but after a short period the workings were abandoned for reasons unknown. It was during the 1860's that cottages were built on the Square, Beddau, and in 1865, the old Beddau Post Office and two cottages were built. The oldest cottages are known as Back Cottages, while the shops were also three cottages during this time. These houses together with the Gelynog Inn and Bethania Baptist Chapel comprised Beddau in 1868.

By 1876, Bute Cottage and Cartref were built by Daniel Price, Esq. (1841-1927) who came from Brecon and was a haulage contractor. The year 1881 saw the building of the two Penybryn cottages, near the Gelynog Inn. From this year until 1912 there was no further expansion. Three private houses were erected in 1915-18, during the first World War, "Delfryn", "Ty Twarch" and "Holly House" and two shops were built by Thomas Edmunds, Esq. Where the four cart tracks met, stood a beech tree and a post on which an oil lamp was hung by the landlord of the Gelynog Inn. He was paid two shillings and sixpence a week. Nearby stood a large iron refuse bin which was emptied once a week. The small community had but one shop and everything was sold there. The owner was Mrs. Elizabeth Watkins popularly known as "Granny Watkins". She remained in charge of the shop until the early thirties. Her husband, Hezekiah Watkins, was a blacksmith and had his workshop where the Gelynog Hotel garages now stand. It is not known how old the Gelynog Hotel is, but it is known to have had a thatched roof and that the owner in 1871, Richard Jones was eligible for voting, the inn having a rateable value of £12 a year. This was the voting qualification then.

The original name was Ty'r Gelynog (which is derived from Celynog meaning Holly). The garden was once surrounded by holly bushes. Holly House may have taken its name from the inn. By 1871, the house was the Gelynog Inn. When the house was altered in 1899-1900, the walls were in a very bad condition. The end wall fell down and in the wall a bag of marbles was found. The inn once boasted its own brew-house but this was removed when the second alteration took place in 1920-21. Hours of opening were 6 a.m. to 10 p.m. continuous! It was also possible to have a drink on Sunday because Beddau was a rural district and outside the three-mile limit of Pontypridd. Drinks could be served to bona-fide travellers. The licence was held for 53 years (1896-1949) by the Harris family who now reside in Llantwit Fardre.

When the school opened in 1877, the building was a great advantage to the community. During the evenings, concerts were held for the entertainment and enjoyment of the inhabitants. The only other place of relaxation was the Gelynog Inn. It was very difficult to make a living during the turn of the century because of lack of numbers in the village. In order to increase trade, rabbit coursing, pony racing and pigeon shooting matches were arranged and would draw large crowds. Many pony and foot races were run along the present Llantrisant Road. The prize would be a barrel of beer. Just before and after the first World War, Enoch Jenkins was one of the competitors in the clay pigeon shooting matches. He was a shot for the English Team and was Champion shot of England. He fired thirteen centuries without a miss! William Price of Bute Cottage was another well known character. He would occasionally ride into the Gelynog Inn on a Penny Farthing bicycle.

Further enjoyment was to be found in Bethania Chapel which was the first religious building in the village (1867). Socials and Penny Readings were held. There were also similar gatherings in Castellau Chapel. Transport was almost non-existent. If one didn't own a horse and trap, it was necessary to walk everywhere. The nearest stations were Llantwit or Cross Inn. Many people walked to Pontypridd for shopping and entertainment. Plays could be seen at the " Royal Clarence Theatre " (County Cinema) or in 1900-1 Wadbrook's pictures outside the New Inn and where the Park Cinema once stood. In Butcher's Yard, there was an entertainment of " living pictures " called Poole's Myrama in 1910. A pleasurable outing, amounting almost to a sensation, would be to walk to Llantrisant to a shed near the Wheatsheaf Hotel and watch Charlie Usher of Cardiff sell fish, his stall being lit by flares.

In these early years, an interesting character lived in Beddau who was one of the sinkers of Cwm Colliery in 1912. His name was Jacob Watkins (1856-1927). He was connected with a memorable event when he and another character named Johnson of Penycoedcae had a race on which was a wager of £5. The event was known as the " Penycoedcae Derby " and has been recorded in verse: —

THE PENYCOEDCAE DERBY (1908)

Why should we think of bygone days
And talk of ancient runners,
When here in Beddau is a man
Who is open to all comers.

That is all comers of his age
For he is well over fifty,
He's not a bird in a gilded cage
But a man who is straight and thrifty.

Yes Jacob Watkins is his name
And I'll tell you of the race,
When he beat Johnson by four yards
And shewed his fastest pace.

That day we never shall forget
Old Jacob's whole limbs trembled,
But beneath all that we saw a look
As to say I'll do or die.

Now Johnson has a record got
Of which he might be proud,
Great races he has won a lot
In fact an awful crowd.

Before the race they rubbed him down
With flesh gloves and with whisky,
They thought to prime him for the fray
And make him bold and frisky.

Ten bob to eight on Johnson
Was the cry all o'er the field,
They thought it was a certainty
That Jacob's doom was sealed.

The pistol went and Johnson gained a clear lead
To begin t'was neck and neck for eighty yards,
Each one must say the men ran hard
It was a glorious race.

Now Jacob ever muscle strained
In fact he meant to win,
Jacob was unkind
And left his man behind.

The crowd went wild
As the tape was shortly breasted,
So Jacob is the winner boys
And with him the laurels rested.

The Beddau hats went in the air
And mad went old Jack Harris,
I thought it was an Irish fair
Or a boozy night in Paris.

In future years
And perhaps our children will often hear,
How Jacob won
The Penycoedcae Derby.

The year 1909 saw the beginnings of the rapid development of the village of Beddau. The first turf was cut on the site of the Cwm Colliery by Mrs. C. H. James, the wife of the Managing Director of the Great Western Colliery Company, in the presence of notable persons including Lady Margaret and Lady Mildred Bramwell of Tir-Mab-Ellis. A tea was held after the ceremony, near the Brickworks, Parish Road, Tynant. From 1909 to 1915 work continued until a shaft was sunk.

The Cwm Pit was sunk by a Yorkshire company for the Great Western Company, who also owned the Maritime Colliery, Pontypridd. Isaac Davies was the contractor. Other men connected with the sinking of the colliery, were Bill Eason, Jacob Watkins, Pryce Hardwicke, Richard Jones, Harry Bressington and Aneurin Williams.

The scope of the original undertaking was commented on in the press:—

"*The new undertaking will be comprised of two shafts* 150 *ft. apart and each sunk to a depth of* 700 *yards. The No.* 1 *or downcast pit will be* 24*ft.* 6 *ins. in diameter and fitted with large cages, carrying four trams on one deck, winding about* 6 *tons of coal on each wind, the loading and unloading to be done automatically, top and bottom, and special arrangements will be made in regard to the guide ropes. The headgear framing will be a large steel designed structure,* 70*ft. high and weighing about* 120 *tons. The No.* 2 *or up-cast pit will be* 20*ft. clean in diameter, fitted with double deck cages, to be used principally for winding men. The colliery is designed to deal with an output of* 3,000 *tons of coal per day with a minimum amount of labour, the motive power to be principally by electric transmission.*

The first woman to descend the pit was Mrs. Tom Owen, Parish Road, Tynant, who made the journey on Christmas Day, 1913. A well-known employee at the Cwm was John Hughes, composer of the hymn tune *Cwm Rhondda.* The first manager was Isaac Rees, Esq.

The colliery was acquired by the Powell Duffryn Company in 1928 and worked by them until the mines were nationalised in 1947.

In 1931, an underground roadway linking the Maritime Colliery near Pontypridd with Cwm was made. In 1957 a similar stone roadway ($3\frac{1}{2}$ miles long) linked Cwm with Coedely. Many projects have been undertaken to improve the mine but the main plans for reorganisation and development of the Cwm Colliery were approved by the National Coal Board in 1951. Coal output has been maintained while the improvements and extensions were being made. The Margaret Shaft is equipped with a skip winder, which is one of the largest in the world, designed for manual or automatic control and is capable of lifting 12 tons of coal at a speed of 26 miles an hour. The Mildred downcast shaft—which in diameter is one of the largest in Europe—augmented by the downcast shafts of Coedely and Maritime, provides ventilation for the combined mine. At Cwm the men are completely under cover from the time they enter the baths when they come to work until they go underground. The canteen, the baths, lamp room and pithead are linked by completely air-conditioned walkways, so that the men are protected from the weather.

Since 1957, there has been a coke ovens and by-products plant at Cwm. It is designed to centralise and maintain production of South Wales foundry coke. The coal mined here is most suitable for foundry coke because of its low sulphur content.

New plant was installed at Cwm in September 1971 at a cost of £293,000. This is used for drying and grinding breeze. The installation was completed in August 1972. Cwm is the National Coal Board's largest coke foundry and plant, comprising 108 ovens processing 552,000 tons of coal a year, mainly from Cwm and Coedely Collieries to produce 424,000 tons of coke. The new installation comprises a rotary drum drier, a rod mill, storage bunkers, conveyors, and weight-feeders. Production commenced in the autumn of 1972 and approximately 75 tons of crushed breeze per day are manufactured.

All sections of the Cwm Coke Ovens and By-Product Plant are fully mechanised.

The year 1870 is a very important one in the history of education. It was during this year that the government made provision for the building of State Schools for the first time. The Education Act also stated that the state schools were to be governed by school boards elected by the ratepayers. Beddau school was built after this Act became law, at a cost of £1,210 3s. 9d., and was opened on 3rd September, 1877. The first headmaster, Mr. Rees Morgan, has recorded his account of the first morning:—

> "*Sept.* 3*rd,* 1877: *This school was opened on Monday, Sep.* 3*rd. Owing to the inclemency of the weather the attendance was materially obstructed. Fifty eight pupils present in the morning with an addition of six in the afternoon. As the children came in I made a rough judgment of their efficiency, judging chiefly by age. The afternoon was devoted to a more minute examination classifying them for registration. Found that a P. Teacher should be engaged as early as possible. The Rev. J. Powell Jones, B.D., Chairman of the Board paid us a visit.*"

Rees Morgan was brought up at Ystradberwig Isaf. He also attended University from there and became first Headmaster of Pontypridd Boys Grammar School.

Before Beddau school was opened, Llantrisant had the only school for this area. The school at Llantrisant was conducted with the aid of voluntary subscriptions and was held at the old Town Hall and Corn Market. As Beddau school was situated in an extra rural area, the headmaster was almost a law unto himself and, according to records, closed the school for reasons which would now be considered unimportant.

During the early nineteenth century, Joseph Lancaster, who was a Quaker, developed a cheap method of education. He used monitors to teach the younger pupils. Monitors were usually chosen from the older pupils. When Beddau school opened it was found necessary to make use of the monitorial system:—

> "*Sep.* 10*th.* 1877: *Engaged Edward Rees as paid monitor and arranged with seven of the first class boys to take charge of a class alternatively. Found this a great assistance.*"

After the school had been opened a fortnight, Monday, Sept. 17th. 1877, "*was set apart as an appointed day by a committee interested in the success of the school to favour children with a treat of tea and cake and a miscellaneous concert in the evening."*

During this period, pupils had to pay fees when they attended school. Pupils at Beddau were obliged to pay twopence a week. When the fee book had to be inspected, the headmaster closed the school so that he could journey to Pontypridd to meet the Government Inspector.

Each year, Her Majesty Victoria's Inspectors visited the school to examine the pupils. It was according to the examination results that the school was paid a government grant for Equipment. On 21st December, 1878, the inspectors reported *"This new school has been well started, a most creditable first examination having been passed. Grant claimable in full £84 which was for* 14 *months."* The Report of 27th June, 1897 was equally flattering: *"A highly satisfactory improvement has taken place in the discipline and attainments of this school."*

A later entry in the records sheds more light on the payment by results system:

8th August, 1881:

Grant as follows:—

	£	s	d
21 exercises marked "Fair" @ 1/-	1	1	0.
8 exercises marked "Good" @ 1/6		12	0.
2 exercises marked "Ex" @ 2/6		5	0.
	1	18	0.
Given by Dept. if 21 earn grants	1	0	0.
	2	18	0.
Spoiled papers @ 1d. each = 34		2	10.
Total Amt. of Grant =	2	15	2.

By 1902, the school grant was £112.

Inspection day was a very special occasion with pupils dressing in their best suits and special preparation on the part of the teacher. An entry in the records dated 4th June, 1895, gives a list of the items the school sang to the inspectors:—

Songs prepared for the Inspection

1. *Inspection Day*
2. *Sleighing Glee*
3. *Dreamland*
4. *O'er the Sea*
5. *Believe me if all those endearing young charms.*

Due to the examination system of this time, the lessons given to children were: Reading, Writing and Arithmetic with a little drawing and needlework for variety.

Before 1880 attendance was not compulsory at school and this fact, naturally led to fluctuating attendance. Also, any event in the district was sufficient to close the school for a holiday:—

Nov. 20th, 1877:

"Gave the children a half-holiday in the afternoon owing to the Reopening of Castellau Chapel"

Or May 12th, 1878:

"——— dismissed children before time on account of Llantrisant fair."

Llantrisant had four fairs during the year and there was also the St. Mary Hill Fair on 26th August. The summer holidays were given for the month of July. Beddau, being an agricultural district, meant that children would be kept home from school during harvest time.

The popular saying "Boys will be boys" was certainly true even in 1877:—

Nov. 16th.

"Punished 7 boys by detaining them after school hours for leaving the school premises and joining a company of huntsmen during the dinner hour and part of the afternoon."

Perhaps the most daring escapade was the one recorded for 14th Dec. 1877:—

"This being the last week but one before Xmas, some of the bigger children made an attempt to lock me out at the time of assembling in the afternoon with a view to obtaining a week's extra holidays. It being the first offence the offenders were let free with a serious caution."

On 7th May, 1878:—

"Enoch Thomas was also punished the second time for robbing a bird's nest of eggs."

A favourite pastime of young boys was to steal a donkey and hitch it to a cart and push them down Castellau Hill.

Holidays were not as long at the end of last century as they are at present, but with school closing, at the discretion of the headmaster for "inclement weather", "tea parties at Penycoedcae", "Castellau Chapel eisteddfodau" and religious meetings, "ploughing matches at Castellau", fairs at Llantrisant and various other reasons, the pupils seemed to have a great advantage. One occasion is of special interest.

On 13th January, 1879:—

"The roads were quite impassable for children—immense snow-drifts, 15 *boys turned up—dismissed them and headmaster gave teachers a lesson in the classroom."*

In the small rural community such as Beddau was, the headmaster was a very important man. He even punished pupils for out of school activities. By 1920, the school population increased and it was necessary to conduct part of the school in the shop, now occupied by the Post Office. Population increased further, and the school population overflowed into St. John's Church and into Zion English Baptist Church, Tynant. On the 12th June, 1922, a " new boys' School " was opened by Mrs. Gwilym Williams, Miskin Manor. The children were given sweets and chocolates in honour of the occasion. The school's motto is "Trwy Lafur Daw Hawddfyd" (Through Labour will come Prosperity). The first headmaster was Thomas H. Pritchard, Esq., who had become headmaster of the old Board School in 1911. Mr. Pritchard had succeeded Rees Morgan, headmaster (1877-1880) and Mr. William Chubb, headmaster (1880-1911). Mr. Pritchard remained headmaster until 1933, D. S. Williams, Esq., was headmaster from 1949 to 1958. D. G. Bonner, Esq., continued in this building known as Castellau Junior School until 1968 when the school moved to Llwyn crwn Primary School. On his retirement in 1979 Mrs. Mary Patricia Jones became headmistress.

By 1928, Beddau's school population had increased so much that a new school was opened on 2nd February, 1931, as Beddau Senior School with D. R. Dawkins, Esq., M.A. (1931-1959) as the first headmaster who was followed by R. W. Francis, Esq., B.Sc. (1960-70) a member of the original staff of 1931. The present headmaster J. G. Lloyd, Esq., B.Sc. succeeded in 1970. The school motto was " Gwybodoeth sydd Nerth " (Knowledge is Strength). From 1950 the school became known as Bryn Celynnog Secondary School. In 1970 the Castellau Junior School was demolished and a new school built in preparation for comprehensive education. Bryn Celynnog Comprehensive School was started in September 1972 and was officially opened on Tuesday, 13th March, 1973 by County Alderman William John Lewis, J.P., of Beddau. The school has a full range of science laboratories, craft rooms, facilities in the creative arts and physical education, a theatre workshop, an advanced language laboratory, library and a youth wing building which contains a lounge and coffee bar which is available as a sixth form common room. The new school motto is " Hunan Ddisgyblaeth " (Self Discipline). The school crest was interpreted by Dillwyn Lewis, history master at Bryn Celynnog Secondary School at that time and designed by Daniel M. Davies, art master at the school.

It represents:—

The five keys of St. Illtud represent Youth, Learning, Chivalry, Priesthood and Knighthood.

The Lion Rampant—part of the arms of the ancient land-owning families of Talbot and Mathew.

The Three Chevrons—the insignia representing Glamorgan.

The Holly Leaves—commemorating the ancient name of the area —Park Gulunog.

First Bus of Edwards Bros., Beddau, 1923

Mount Pleasant Church Sisterhood Outing, 1927

First Sunday School Outing of St. Michael and All Angels' Church, Beddau, 1936

The Welfare Quoits Team, 1935/36

Beddau Tableaux that took part at a Peace Rally in Pontypridd, 1935

Zion E.B. Chapel, Tynant, 1921

Cwm Welfare Football Team, 1945

Cwm Canteen Committee and Staff, 1941-1953

Members of the Bryn Celynnog School Brass Band in Investiture Year 1969
(*Photograph by the Celtic Press*)

The ultra-modern Church of St. Michael and All Angels, b. 1936. Restored 1966

Rev. J. V. Payne, B.A. with Churchwardens and Choir at Beddau Church, 1949

Beddau Centenary Celebrations Committee, 1965

Unveiling the Plaque, Centenary Gardens, Beddau, Sunday, 1st March, 1970.
L. to R.—Mrs. Barbara Davies (*Treasurer*), Mr. Dewi Bonner (*Chairman*), Coun. K. Pontin (*Chairman, L.R.D.C.*), Lt.-Col. J. R. L. Traherne, *High Sheriff of Glamorgan,* Mr. Dillwyn Lewis (*Secretary*), Rev. Edwin Davies, B.A., *Vicar of Llantrisant*

Last Pontypridd and Llantrisant Divisional Executive for Education
Glamorgan Education Committee, March 1974

ELIZABETH THE SECOND

by the Grace of God of the United Kingdom of Great Britain and Northern Ireland and of Our other Realms and Territories Queen, Head of the Commonwealth, Defender of the Faith:

TO ALL TO WHOM THESE PRESENTS SHALL COME, GREETING!

WHEREAS certain new local government areas known as districts have been established by the Local Government Act 1972:

AND WHEREAS a Petition praying for the grant of a Charter conferring upon the district of Taff-Ely the status of a borough has been presented unto Us by the council of the said district:

AND WHEREAS We are pleased by the advice of Our Privy Council to grant a Charter for such purpose.

NOW THEREFORE KNOW YE that We, by virtue of Our Prerogative Royal and in pursuance of the Local Government Act 1972 and of all other powers and authorities enabling Us in that behalf, have granted and declared and by these Presents do grant and declare that the district of Taff-Ely shall have the status of a borough.

This Our Charter shall not take effect before the first day of April, One thousand nine hundred and seventy-four.

IN WITNESS whereof We have caused these Our Letters to be made Patent.

WITNESS Ourself at Westminster the twenty-seventh day of February in the twenty-third year of Our Reign.

Borough of Taff Ely Charter ganted 1974

LLANTRISANT AND LLANTWIT FARDRE R.D.C., 1974

Back Row—H. S. Davies; R. W. Thomas; K. Williams, Dep. Treasurer; J. Gardines, Dep. Surveyor; W. R. Jacob; S. Balby; T. John; J. A. Copeland; R. J. Brown, Treasurer.

Middle Row—R. A. Huxton, Dep. Clerk; T. J. Hopkins, Surveyor; S. G. Flower; D. J. Harrison; K. Roderick; K. Ponting; I. Hughes; S. Mason, P.H.INS.

Front Row—Dr. Eileen G. Watkins, M.O.H.; Dr. W. Moody Jones; Mrs. A. G. Herbert; R. J. Selwood, Vice-Chairman; L. L. Carter, J.P., Chairman; W. J. Maddocks, Clerk; T. W. Roderick; R. Cox.

First School photograph of Pupils at the new Beddau Board School, 1878

Soup Kitchen at the Brickwork, Tynant during a strike, May 1921

Tynant Wesleyan Guild at Ogmore, 1927

Headmaster Mr. T. Pritchard and Staff of Beddau Board School, 1920

Headmistress Miss Ann David and Staff of Beddau Infants' School, 1927

First Headmaster Mr. D. R. Dawkins, M.Sc. and Staff
of Bryn Celynnog Secondary School, 1932

First Headmaster Mr. J. G. Lloyd, B.Sc. and Staff of Bryn Celynnog Comprehensive, 1972

Palmer's Bus. Beddau—Pontypridd route, 1921

A tradition which has continued with the new school is the successful Bryn Celynnog School Brass Band. The band was formed in 1964 and has numerous activities. They include appearances on T.V., and an annual celebrity concert. They have also appeared with Semprini, the well-known pianist. The band has won the Open Youth Brass Band Championships of Great Britain at Liverpool on three occasions. Through its varied and numerous activities including appearances on T.V., the band has become well-known and has added to the musical life of the district under the able and distinctive direction of Ieuan Morgan, Esq., and Anthony F. Moore, Esq.

The old Board School continued to serve the educational needs of the village as part of the Comprehensive School, but the school finally closed in December 1981. Also the original school canteen, opened in 1949, was closed in 1981. Since 1922 this school was the Infants Department with Miss Ann David as headmistress (1922-47), succeeded by Miss Minnie Harris (1947-64), Miss Gwyneth Dickason became headmistress in 1964 and moved from Castellau Infants School to a new building in 1968 known as Delfryn Infants School. With the development of the village it was necessary to build yet another school. Gwaun Meisgyn Primary School received the first children in January 1972 and was officially opened by County Councillor Kelvin Eason, on Tuesday, 3rd April, 1973. The school has been built in the modern open-plan style. Miss Gwyneth Dickason, J.P., was the first headmistress. In 1978 Gwaun Meisgyn became a Junior School with Mr. Trevor Goulden as headmaster and Miss Dickason as first headmistress of the new Gwaun Meisgyn Infants Nursery School. Mr. Goulden was headteacher until 1981.

In 1921 the modern village of Beddau was built and with the growing community came the need for the Church.

Although people living in the hamlet already held some meetings in houses or the Beddau Board School, the only religious building was Bethania Chapel built in 1867 and used first by the Baptists then by the Church of England when the Rev. Daniel Fisher, Curate of Llantrisant, held services at Beddau.

He held a service at Beddau at the school on Sunday, 1st August, 1897, when he dedicated an harmonium for use at services which also commemorated Queen Victoria's Diamond Jubilee. By 1913 Bethania became Baptist once more and by 1921 a new larger Baptist Chapel was dedicated and lasted until 1968 when it was demolished.

Members worshipped in the original building which had been restored and re-dedicated by Rev. C. M. Thomas, in September 1967. The honour of opening the newly restored chapel was given to Mrs. Harriet Jones a founder-member of Bethania. This chapel was completely demolished in February 1974 and a new chapel is planned for part of the site opened in 1975. The contractor is Stuart Cook, Esq., a great-grandson of William Williams, Ty Cwrdd, Castellau.

Among the names of the trustees of the 1921 Church was John Hughes of Tonteg, who found fame as the composer of the hymn-tune *Cwm Rhondda*. The Rev. C. M. Thomas was the first minister of the church, 1958-78. A new chapel was opened in 1976.

The need for places of religious worship increased. The first churches in Tynant were meetings held in houses. The Wesleyan Methodists, Spiritualists and Salvation Army all held meetings there. Out of these beginnings to establish churches in Beddau and Tynant, Zion Baptist Church made a firm hold and flourished over the years.

The church began one Sunday in 1919 when six lay-preachers by the names of Messrs. Prosser, Morgan, Williams, Parry, Roberts and Thorne, came from Cardiff and held a meeting in the open air at Tynant.

Meetings continued to be held in houses and on 21st October, 1921, Zion Church as we know it today was opened. The building was originally an army hut of World War I and has given excellent service for 50 years.

A choir conducted by Tom Owen Esq. was formed and the Church was opened by Dr. Edwards, Principal of the Baptist College, Cardiff, at the time. Zion is famous locally for its anniversary services which were conducted by Mr. Harry Wright of Tynant and Mrs. O. Roberts, Woodlands, accompanying the choir.

Many have served this church faithfully in the past but at the present time there is no minister. The affairs of the church are conducted by the secretary, Mr. Bert Morris, who has been a member for over 50 years, Mr. W. A. Boaden, treasurer, whose family has served faithfully the cause at Zion, Miss K. Head, Deaconess and Mr. Jenkin Davies, Senior Deacon.

One or the most attractive buildings in Beddau is St. Michael and All Angels Church. This was built in ultra-modern style in 1936.

Like other religious causes the Church found it necessary to have a home of its own. The Vicar of Llantrisant, the Rev. D. T. Griffiths, finally settled on a building which was located at Gilfach Goch and was of iron construction.

The church at Gilfach was using part of this large structure. The other part was transported to Beddau and opened as St. John's Church in 1921. The Rev. J. O. Williams, Curate of Llantrisant, conducted services here. He became the first Vicar of Gilfach Goch and after resided at the Vicarage, Llantwit Feardref with his son, the Rev. A. Williams, where he died in January 1973. Originally the iron building in Gilfach Goch was used as sleeping quarters for navvies who were building Garden Village, and it later fell into disuse.

With part used as the church at Beddau the building left in Gilfach was purchased by a Mr. Johnny Rosser, who kept it as a billiards hall and shop. The cost of the church building when purchased was £60 and Llantrisant Parish paid the cost.

This building was the Church Hall at Beddau, but became derelict and the building was demolished in 1973. The new church was dedicated on Thursday, 30th July, 1936, by the Rt. Rev. Dr. Timothy Rees, Bishop of Llandaff.

The new building was initiated in the first instance by Lt. Col. Sir Rhys-Williams, Bart., K.C., D.S.O., and Lady Juliet Rhys-Williams of Miskin Manor.

For a religious building, it is certainly unusual, if not unique. The original structure was remodelled in 1966. The design and the colouring of the church are intended to symbolise three things, namely: the Incarnation of Christ, the History of Mankind, and the Life of each individual.

The first curate in charge was the Rev. D. H. Hughes, who left in 1940 to be succeeded by the Rev. J. V. Payne, who stayed until 1949, and who is now Rural Dean and Vicar of Pontypridd.

The Rev. John Fluke (d. Jan. 1982) served 1950-57 succeeded by the Rev. G. Horwood, Rev. M. R. Ellis, Rev. John Flowers, Rev. J. Binney, Rev. P. Ryan, Rev. Morley R. Morgan and Rev. Wyn Beynon.

The new church at Beddau attracted visitors from all over the world. In the visitor's book one signature is recorded of a world-famous novelist—Elinor Glyn. She was known as the foremost romantic novelist of her time and was the mother of Lady Juliet Rhys-Williams of Miskin Manor.

The church was licensed for the Solemnisation of Marriage and Publication of Banns on 1st February, 1948, and the first wedding took place on 6th March, 1948.

Lady Rhys-Williams continued to visit the church annually on its anniversary until her death in 1964. The church is still part of the Parish of Llantrisant under the spiritual guidance of the Vicar, the Rev. Edwin Davies, B.A.

Another place of worship which has played an important part in Beddau communal life is Mount Pleasant. The original chapel was opened in November 1924, but the first meetings were in private houses and later in the Beddau School. There was no actual denomination decided until the chapel was built. The church then became devoted to the cause of the Presbyterian Church in Wales, also known as the Forward Movement. The first minister was Rev. John Badham, Llantwit Fardre and he remained with the church until 1939, when the Rev. A. G. Thomas became minister.

The new minister did not have a church for long because one night in May, 1940, a great tragedy occurred that was to deprive members and Beddau of a popular, flourishing church. Improvements were being made to Mount Pleasant Park and near the church stood a tractor and petrol. Somehow sparks from the tractor developed and the result was a big burnt-out framework of Mount Pleasant Chapel. Valiant efforts were made by the Fire Brigade and villagers to rescue as much of the furniture as possible. Although Beddau had bombs during enemy raids, the burning of Mount Pleasant Chapel was perhaps the greatest tragedy of the war. Members of the church found many willing helpers and held meetings in the Church Hall and later in the schools. Adult members met in Trinity Chapel, Llantwit Fardre. After the War, Beddau had a Mount Pleasant Chapel again. A new church was opened in

November 1946. The present minister is the Rev. D. J. Howells, who came to Mount Pleasant in 1946. The church celebrated its jubilee in 1974. The Rev. Howells retired to Aberystwyth in 1976. The church closed for services in 1977.

The youngest religious cause to be established in Beddau, is the Assemblies of God (Full Gospel Mission). The first meetings were held in a dance hall at the rear of Bute Cottage by a travelling evangelist named William Lewis of Wallasey in 1936. Several persons were convinced of the beliefs of this religious cause. By 1940, the members had a church of their own. In 1946, misfortune overtook the church and it was burned down. The church members struggled on and their faith was rewarded when a second church was established in 1948. The present building was a gift to the Beddau Church from a church at Tongwynlais.

Beddau has, from earliest times, been an area on which battles have been fought. Industry brought its own problems and a new kind of battle. During 1921, there was a strike in the Cwm Colliery because of a policy of reduction in wages. Wages had been high during the First World War, but now the government sought to reduce wages. During the war, colliers were being paid five shillings a day, but by 1939, wages were two pounds, seventeen shillings a week. Because of the strike, people had to be fed by means of soup kitchens which were located at the brickworks in Parish Road.

Opposite Zion stands the bakehouse which was built in 1925. Many people took their bread and cakes to be cooked there, especially at Christmas time, when trade was heavy and on Christmas morning itself, turkeys and chickens were cooked there. Due to food restrictions during the war, trade declined and the bakehouse closed in 1942.

By 1926, the General Strike engulfed the nation and Beddau was described as a distressed area. Back came the soup kitchens in a field near the Gelynog Hotel and meals were given in the assembly rooms of the hotel. Children were fed in the hall of Mount Pleasant Chapel, while adults were looked after at the hotel. Once a fortnight, a loaf, butter and a little cheese were distributed around the houses. The District Council paid food bills.

Conditions were so serious that many wonder how they lived through this period in their lives. Help was sought from the Lord Mayor of London's Fund so that clothes could be obtained for children and adults. During school time the children were helped by the teachers who distributed shoes to all children who needed them. During this difficult period, Miss Ann David, headmistress of Beddau School and Mr. Thomas Pritchard, headmaster helped in organising relief to the community with the secretary, Mr. Evan Roberts. Many other inhabitants also tried to do their best, especially towards the children. Many families left Beddau at this time for England where there was chance of employment. In 1936, the government of the day inaugurated a scheme to ensure employment in the distressed areas of South Wales. The result was the Treforest Industrial Estate which now employs many hundreds of people from our district. The Estate was officially opened by the Duke of Kent in July 1936.

Work began slowly, but in June 1927, the Cwm Colliery was closed because of a trade depression. The colliery was now managed by the Powell Duffryn Coal Company. The colliery had originally been sunk by the Great Western Company. Workmen found themselves once more with only a few shillings on which to live. To collect the money, it was necessary to go to the New Inn at Llantwit Fardre. The colliery reopened at Eastertime 1929.

Life continued to be hard and it was difficult to hold a job. During the election in 1928, people were so poor that many were obliged to wait until evening when it was dark and then go to vote, dressed in a neighbour's coat because their poverty did not allow them to own a coat. Meetings were always being held and in 1926, at the Gelynog Hotel, a plain-clothes policeman was found to be hiding in the audience. He was discovered and the angry crowd forcibly ejected him. Policemen always kept a look-out and often chased men who were picketing workmen.

Although times were difficult, many concerts were organised for funds and jazz bands were formed. The Cwm Colliery had a Silver Band founded by John Thomas who had come to live in Tynant from Cwmparc, Rhondda. He was popularly known as 'John the Band'. The supporters walked with the bands to Cardiff and elsewhere when the bands were performing. Mostly, concerts were connected with the places of worship and held in their several buildings. In 1925, the workmen started paying twopence a week towards a fund which would eventually provide them with an institute. After much hard work during an unstable period, sufficient money had been collected to make an application to the Colliery Welfare Scheme for a loan. This was done in 1930. On 11th August, 1932, two foundation stones were laid by D. L. Davies, Esq., Member of Parliament for the Pontypridd Constituency, and Mr. A. G. Brown, agent of the colliery.

The institute is situated in the centre of the village of Beddau-Tynant on a site given by the Powell Duffryn Coal Company and was opened on Saturday, 21st October, 1933. It is built of brick faced with cement and has slated roofs. The hall originally seated 450 persons (the hall was extended in 1956, and now seats 516 persons). There is a stage and dressing rooms which are now connected to the Lesser Hall at the rear. The Lesser Hall was opened in September 1949 by Arthur Pearson, Esq., Member of Parliament and H. McVicar, Esq., M.E. The institute portion of the building includes a billiards room, a reading room, and a library. The whole building and furnishings cost just over £5,000. Surrounding the hall are lawns and flower gardens, which have received years of loving care from the gardeners.

On the opening evening, there was a free concert and several of the musical items were by artistes who had won awards in the Welsh National Eisteddfod. Artistes listed in the ceremonial programme are:

Madam Chubb, Contralto

Madam Myfanwy Jones, Elocutionist
Madam Blodwen Edwards, Soprano
Mr. Dewi Chubb, Bass
Mr. Fred Porter, Tenor.

In the foreword written to the programme, it is stated that:

> " *This building is of more than usual interest because it took the Committee several years of hard, unremitting endeavours to realise their ambition—a period during which such set-backs were encountered that only unusual patience and faith succeeded in eventually combating.*"

It was also hoped that the new hall would exert a profound cultural influence on the lives of all who used it.

The first manager of the hall was Evan Roberts, Esq., a man who had worked with his neighbours during the difficult days of hardship and strikes. During his administration, live entertainment was presented at the hall. The first entertainment was given by Ted and May Hopkins who were very famous in 1933 and had toured theatres all over Britain. Today their names are legendary and their recordings of monologues and duologues such as " Treorchy Fair ", " The Welsh Courtship ", " The Welsh Maid " and " The Squire " are sought after by collectors.

Short seasons of plays were presented by the James James Players. Several well-known plays were given including such standards as "Maria Marten and the Red Barn ", " The Maid of Cefn Ydfa ", " Uncle Tom's Cabin " while on Saturdays, pantomimes like " Cinderella " and " Jack and the Beanstalk " were presented at matinees.

After a struggle to keep the hall open, the inevitable happened. Films came to Beddau. The hall was then re-named The Gaiety Cinema and continued as a cinema ever since, live entertainment taking the stage only occasionally. Films were first shown to the public in a dance hall at the rear of Bute Cottage in 1932. Previous to this date the building had been used for dances and whist drives. The hall was not used after 1946. In 1956 the Gaiety Cinema was extended and the stage remodelled to accommodate the modern CinemaScope screen. The cinema closed in June 1964. The hall has had several managers during its existence:—

Evan Roberts, Esq. (1933-1935)
Secretary to Welfare Committee 1924-1946.
Frank Calcutt, Esq. (1935-1937)
Idris Evans, Esq. (1939-1946)
Cyril Taylor, Esq. (1937-1939)
L. C. Hughes, Esq. (1946-1951)
Arthur R. Crook, Esq. (1951-1953)
William Snelgrove, Esq. (1953-1972)
Trevor Williams, Esq. (1972-1973)
Bryn Williams, Esq.
Thomas Hughes, Esq.
Kenneth Porter, Esq.

The Welfare Hall is now a successful Social Club.

While the Welfare Hall has catered for film fans and dancers, concerts of various types and boxing matches have also been held here. Boxing matches were also held in the Dance Hall, The Square, Beddau. Here, William Price sponsored Panther Purches and Cuthbert Taylor who were very famous during the thirties. Some of Tommy Farr's first fights were also sponsored by Mr. Price. The wonder of television came to the village in 1952.

Progress was slow in many other matters but it was not possible to bring up-to-date facilities quickly because of the difficult times the community had experienced. A clinic had been held there since 1924 in the Lesser Hall of Mount Pleasant and remained there until 1939 when the new clinic was opened. The fact that Beddau had a clinic at all was due to the work of a voluntary committee of women including Mrs. Noah Smith, with Mrs. Evan Roberts as supervisor of the supplies of food. The doctor's surgery was held in a private house supervised by Doctor Washington Evans, Llantwit. Beddau now has a modern surgery building supervised by Doctor Wakelin, who has taken over from Doctor Washington Evans. The surgery was opened in 1956. Doctor Washington Evans (1892-1955) was a native of Pontypridd whose father was a doctor there. He first came to Llantwit Fardre in 1921 (and became Superintendent of St. John's Ambulance and Red Cross and was a Justice of the Peace. In 1955, his partner, Doctor J. H. S. Wakelin took over the practice. During this period William Evans led the Ambulance Team at the Cwm Colliery. Popularly known as 'Evans the Ambulance' he gave many years of devoted service.

Beddau has added to its public amenities. In 1938 the park was opened; in 1940 a health clinic was brought into use; several sports clubs, a youth centre and a large number of organisations all add to the interesting community life of the village. In 1962 the Beddau Rugby Club opened a modern Clubhouse but Rugby Football was first established at Beddau during the mid-twenties. Beddau's star team achieved fame during the 1928-29 period and was almost unbeatable. In 1928 the team played at Cardiff Arms Park on two occasions, firstly in the semi-final of the Mallet Cup when Beddau beat the great Cardiff Scottish team and in the Final of the Mallet Cup against Canton, Cardiff. In recognition of their skill during 1928-29 season, Doctor Washington Evans presented the team with tasselled scarlet velvet caps. The Beddau team was one of the thirteen clubs who joined the Rugby League Union when they started in South Wales with headquarters at Pontypridd. This season, Beddau played in the Final of the Rugby League Cup at Taff Vale Park, Treforest. Interest waned for some years but was renewed by W. R. Harrison, Esq., of Beddau in 1952. He had been a member of the invincible team of 1928 and, although soccer was played on the Mount Pleasant Park ground, he felt that there was interest in Rugby as well. Due to his enthusiasm and hard work he was able to organise a team and the first game was played at Mount Pleasant Park on 6th September, 1952. Mr. Harrison was referee at this game. This was the beginning of Beddau Rugby Club, which has prospered and brought distinction to the village. One of its members, Gareth Prothero, played for Wales in International games and was selected to be a member of the British Lions Touring Team for 1966. In 1965, the club obtained Welsh Rugby Union status.

On 30th November, 1965 Beddau's new modern library was opened by Alderman Theophilus Griffiths of Beddau. The first librarian was Mrs. Christine Reynolds who retired in 1974 after over 25 years' service. This building is a most worthy addition to the amenities of the village. The library also houses the village War Memorial, which was unveiled by the Rev. J. V. Payne, B.A., Vicar of Pontypridd. The Rev. John Payne was curate at Beddau in 1940-49 and was the first Chairman of the War Memorial Committee. The plaque was unveiled on Sunday, 8th May, 1966, the 21st Anniversary of Victory in Europe Day.

Since 1963 there have been substantial housing estate projects sponsored by the Llantrisant and Llantwit Fardre Rural District Council. In 1966 a new private garden village-type housing estate was started on the lands of Llwyncrwn Uchaf Farm. The plans include a shopping precinct and is imaginatively designed, with trees and footpaths which give easy access to all parts of the estate using a collector road system. A new phase of the estate is now under construction which extends almost to Brynteg. Brynteg itself has developed into a pleasant rural residential district.

A large estate has been developed on Gwaun Meisgyn since 1966 and now includes Gwaun Meisgyn Primary School. A new shopping precinct has been built near the school and on 15th October, 1973, a new hostelry, "The Bowman", was opened. The name reminds us of the connection of the Llantrisant area with the Bowmen at the Battle of Crécy. A modern social development is the need for a Day Centre where our Senior Citizens can meet socially in comfortable surroundings. Such a centre was opened at Penyparc on Monday, 7th December, 1981 by Cllr. George Preston, Mayor of Taff-Ely. This amenity is very much appreciated.

During May and June 1965, the village celebrated its Centenary as a community. The event is commemorated by a street of houses called Centenary Court (1966). On Sunday, 1st March, 1970, the Centenary Gardens were officially opened by Lieutenant-Colonel J. R. L. Traherne, K.St.J., D.L., High Sheriff of Glamorgan, who was invited to unveil the commemorative plaque by Councillor K. Pontin, Chairman of the Llantrisant and Llantwit Fardre Rural District Council. The dedication was performed by Rev. Edwin Davies, Vicar of Llantrisant. The Bryn Celynnog School Band, conducted by Mr. A. F. Moore, played a selection of music for the assembled guests. The Centenary Gardens project was realised due to co-operation between the Rural District Council and the Centenary Committee who provided the Centenary Gardens. The Centenary Gardens will be a visible reminder to all of our existence as a community. The design and construction of the gardens was supervised by Mr. T. J. Hopkins, B.Sc., Surveyor to the

Llantrisant and Llantwit Fardre Rural District Council. Mr. John T. Gray and Mr. Michael Melody played a prominent part in designing the gardens.

The Centenary Committee trusts that the Centenary Gardens will give pleasure to all who use them.

The year 1966 was a year of unique honour for the village. The Chairman of the Glamorgan County Council for 1966-67 was County Alderman Theophilus Griffiths who had been a member of the Llantrisant District Council and a member of the County Council since 1940 until he died in October 1967. Together with County Alderman William John Lewis, J.P., he had represented the area in public life. Alderman Lewis retired from the County Council on reorganisation in April 1974 after 50 years of public service having served the area on the Llantrisant Parish and District Councils before becoming a member of the Glamorgan County Council in 1959. He is the first Beddau resident to be made a Justice of the Peace. He has expressed his appreciation of the Llantrisant district in verse:—

MY FRIENDS

From John O'Groats, to Lands End
From Anglesey to Kent,
The people that I like the best
Are those I represent
The good kind people of Tonteg
And Efail Isaf too,
Church Village, Llantwit, and Tynant
I raise my hat to you.

Pencoedcae, Beddau, and Cross Inn
Llantrisant, Talbot Green,
Groesfaen and Miskin, Mwyndy Cross
And all at Pontyclun.
All at Brynsadler, Talygarn
To me you're all my friends,
That friendship I'll appreciate
Till my life's journey ends.

W. J. LEWIS
(Gwilym Llaeron).

He is known as the Bard of County Hall, having composed poetry for several occasions there and throughout Glamorgan. Poems of other current interest like "The men on the Moon" have appeared in the Press. Alderman Lewis is descended from Ieuan Gwyllt, the Welsh bard who translated the Moody and Sankey hymn book into Welsh,

" Swn y Jwbilee " and originated the Cyfanfa Ganu tradition. Here are poems on this district: —

ARDAL CASTELLAU

Mae ardal Castellau
   Fel gwyddoch i gyd,
Yn un o Ardaloedd
   Prydferthaf y Cyd.

Ar Capel bach diddan
   Yn ymyl y Nant,
Yn dal i groesawu
   Hynafgwyr, a Phlant.

Bu adeg yn hanes
   Yr ardal un tro,
Pan oedd yr Eisteddfod
   Yn seinio trwy'r fro,
Ond wir erbyn heddyw
   Daeth hyny i ben,
Nid 'Steddfod geir mwyach
   Ond swn y Top-Ten.

Er hyny hyderwn
   Cawn weled y dydd,
Pan ddaw'r Capel bychan
   O'i rwymau yn rhydd.
A rywbryd efallai
   Er gwaethau'r Top-Ten,
Cawn eto'r Eisteddfod
   A'r hyfryd Amen.

W. J. LEWIS
(Gwilym Llaeron)

LLANTRISANT PARISH CHURCH

Of all the Churches in the land
   There's none that is more pleasant,
Than our Ancient Parish Church
   Up here in Llantrisant.

This fine old Church, built on the rock
   On sure sound foundation
Has served the Parish truly well
   For many a generation.

When strolling through the country-side
   On a fine summer's evening
Oh, what sweet music fills the air
   The old Church Bells are chiming.

In this old Church the people meet
   Within its walls to worship,
Where little Children are Baptized
   And couples end their courtship.

And when Life's Journey's at an end
   For some as we go onward,
A peaceful resting place is found
   For them inside the Church-yard.

W. J. LEWIS
(Gwilym Llaeron)

The new developments in the village continue the spirit of the pioneers whose achievements in education, religious life and welfare have brought improvement. The story of Beddau is the story of achievements of ordinary people realised in difficult and extraordinary periods of economic slump in the twenties and thirties.

22. Efail Castellau

Approximately three quarters of a mile north west of Beddau, is the rural district of Castellau which is dominated by Castellau Fawr, the home of Lieutenant-Colonel J. R. Ll. Traherne, late of the 1st Battalion Welch Regiment. The word Castellau means fortifications and there exists to the north of Castellau Fawr a mound which was once a hill-fort. In Llantrisant Church, Castellau is referred to as "Cist-y-lle", which means chest or coffer. In troubled times the inhabitants of the farming community around about sent their treasures and valuables to the fort and later the mansion for safe keeping.

The Traherne family lived at Castellau Fawr for several centuries. They are descended through Sir George Herbert of Swansea, from the seat of Einon ap Collwyn (temp. William Rufus), Lord of Senghenydd (Caerphilly) and Miskin after the conquest of Glamorgan by the Normans in 1091.

It is not known who built the original house at Castellau, but the Traherne family were there at the end of the sixteenth century and may have built the Tudor portions of the house which are the two north wings. In 1630, the mansion was occupied by Edmund Traherne, Esq., Portreeve of Llantrisant at that time. The house is situated on the side of the old road which was made by Gwrgan, one of the old princes of Glamorgan. The road led from Llantwit Major, the educational centre, to Hirwaun (Wurgan) near Aberdare. The imposing house is situated with a semi-circle of trees and has a fine stretch of park-like grounds extending downwards in a gentle slope from the house to the parish road. The house has the appearance of having at one time occupied a position of importance.

While journeying in South Wales between June and October, 1803. B. H. Makin in "Antiquities of South Wales" describes the scene at Castellau:—

> "*The descent on the northern side of Llantrisant opens to the view of country, where the effects of cultivation are less generally visible, and the less expanded vale partakes the character of the hilly scenery by which it is surrounded. On passing the cleft in which the town stands the change in the face of nature is striking, and the contrast of character between a mountain valley and that which you have just left, rarely impresses itself more strongly on the mind. From this eminence, Castellau a seat belonging to the family of Traherne, is seen to much advantage, and forms, by its appearance, a gay and brilliant spot in a landscape whose prevailing style is grand and sombre, a fortified place, but what bloody scenes have been acted there, it has not been my fortune to discover. Perhaps its retirement within the hills has involved*

it in a peaceful and happy security. At Castellau, various sorts of myrtle bear the open air in the shrubberies all the year round. May not this be considered proof that the mountain climate is not much colder than that of the vale, though for the most part more humid from the mists which frequently collect about the mountains and are condensed into hasty showers, or continued drizzly rains."

In the early eighteenth century, after his marriage with Prudence Williams of Ynysgerwn, Edmund Traherne built the elegant south front of the house with its charming rounded eastern and western ends. The beautiful fireplace in the pillared drawing room dates from this time, also the armorial window which lights the stone spiral staircase. A bell which was rung to assemble the staff of the house still hangs from the side of the house. The Traherne family remained at Castellau until the death of another Edmund in 1808, when the property was sold by his son, Llewelyn Traherne of Coedriglan and St. Hilary. The house then passed to the family of Williams of Aberpergwm (Neath), who during the nineteeenth century resided both at Castellau and Aberpergwm. William Williams of Aberpergwm is lineally descended from Iestyn ap Gwrgant, who was a descendant of Caractacus, Britain's defender against the Romans. It is of interest to know that the mother of Sir Rhys Rhys-Williams, Bart., who was a daughter of the Williams of Aberpergwm, was born at Castellau.

The Williams family, after they had purchased St. Donat's Castle, appear to have abandoned living at Castellau and the house was occupied by a tenant farmer and allowed to go almost to ruin.

During this period cattle were seen to be going in and out of the drawing room and dining room windows. Mr. Emrys Evans purchased Castellau about 1930, and restored the south front. In 1946, the Traherne family purchased Castellau and brought it back into the ownership of the original family. By this time the house had been out of the family's possession for nearly a hundred and forty years. The house was owned by Lieutenant-Colonel J. R. Ll. Traherne until he moved in 1976.

Since retiring from the army in 1959, Colonel Traherne had resided at Castellau and devoted much of his time to local organisations and charities. Since 1962, Colonel John Traherne has been made a Deputy Lieutenant for the County of Glamorgan and Principal Secretary of the Priory for Wales, Order of St. John. In 1966, he was made Chief Commissioner for Wales, and is a Knight of the Order of St. John. Already the Traherne family had provided three High Sheriffs for Glamorgan. During Investiture year of Charles, Prince of Wales, 1969, Lieutenant-Colonel Traherne served as High Sheriff of Glamorgan. The family motto is:—

"Ofna Dduw a'r Brenhin"

(Fear God and the King)

A short distance from the Castellau Mansion stands an inn which was built during the sixteenth century. The house known as the " Lamb and Flag ", was originally called " The Inn ". Where the present car park is situated, a blacksmith's shop stood and opposite the mill which has been converted into garages. In the field next to the mill stood an oast house. The grinding wheels of the mill now form tables in the inn garden. The inn stood on the side of the parish road leading to Llantrisant and was probably a coaching inn during its early days. The mill was kept busy by the many farms in the neighbourhood. Tynant farm always had its grain ground here right up to the early days of the present century. The inn was remodelled in the early twenties and named " Lamb and Flag ". The name has historical connections, the sign of the " Lamb and Flag " is the coat of arms of the Aberpergwm family. Ninety years ago, the house had a thatched roof.

Opposite the " Lamb and Flag " inn lies the Welsh Independent Chapel, Castellau. The chapel was originally built in 1843 and rebuilt and enlarged in 1877. Until 1939, the chapel was the centre of an annual eisteddfod. The brook outside has been used for baptisms. The chapel owes its parentage to the Cymmer Chapel, Porth, the oldest Nonconformist Chapel in the Rhondda, founded in 1738.

Half a mile along the parish road from Castellau towards Llantrisant, stands Ty-Clwyddau. The house dates from the sixteenth century and has an unusual feature in a stone, spiral staircase. At the side of the house stands a gate which marks the extreme limits of Llantrisant Common. The house seems to have been built as a lodge, guarding the interests of Llantrisant Common. The house has been a farm for many years.

Between Treferig and Castellau Mansions stands the ruin of Treferig mill.

Treferig Mill is situated opposite the two cottages known as sawmill cottages, Castellau and Llantrisant. The water to work the mill was taken from the Nant Mychedd stream at a point just below Ty Cwrdd, the old Quaker Meeting House, and then carried in a channel to a pond above the mill. This field is still known as Cae Pond today. It then ran through a culvert under the road into another pond and then through the sluice and over the mill wheel back into the Nant Mychedd stream.

The last miller to grind corn at Treferig mill was Thomas Bussell, who came from Somerset to Cardiff about the year 1830. He walked from Cardiff to Croesfaen and stayed at the Croesfaen Inn for a few days. He found work as a miller at the Abertridwr mill, which he worked for some years. He eventually married a Miss Price, the daughter of the people keeping the Croesfaen Inn at that time. Subsequently he moved to Treferig Mill which he worked for several years.

For some time he also worked a windmill and the water mill at St.-y-nyll, St. Bride's-super-Ely in conjunction with the Treferig Mill. He also worked the mill at Tonyrefail.

Thomas Bussell died at Pantydraenan Farm, Llantrisant in the year 1875, and was buried at St. Martin's Church, Caerphilly.

There was also a timber saw mill which remained active until the early twenties.

Alongside the mill was a railway siding which was the only collecting point for the farmers of the district including Beddau. The farmers just collected their foodstuffs etc. from a rail van which was brought to the siding and left there until all the contents had been disposed of. There was no one to supervise the collections. The farmers just collected the orders on their own account. The Treferig Valley Railway was built in 1878-1879 to service the Glyn Colliery.

The waters of the stream serving the Treferig mill also served Castellau Fach, near which was a rustic summer retreat. In a half hidden nook stood the Baddon or bath-house. It was a huge basin built in the interior near the cool waters of the Treferig stream. Here stood an old house and it is said that in former days it was used as a hospital for those who had fallen wounded in battle.

A short walk from the Baddon is Darren Ddeusdant. The place was supposed to have been a weird sanctuary of the Druids in the open air. There are several crosses cut into the rock.

For what must surely be the first time for a period much longer than within living memory, an interesting ceremony took place at Darren Ddeusant. On Whitsun Monday, 7th June, 1965, a pilgrimage took place led by the Rev. Edwin Davies, B.A., Vicar of Llantrisant, Rev. Malcolm Ellis, B.A., Curate of Llantrisant and Rev. D. J. Howells of Llantwit Fardre. Before going to the Altar Stone, Col. J. R. L. Traherne was presented with a parchment commemorating the occasion.

The address was:—

WHIT-MONDAY PILGRIMAGE, 1965

" *To the Lieutenant-Colonel J. R. L. Traherne of Castellau Fawr we bring greetings. And we request that you will conduct these pilgrims to Darren Ddeusant, where it is commonly believed the Saints of old did preach the Gospel from the ancient preaching stone, and where our forefathers were accustomed to assemble for the praise and worship of Almighty God. Furthermore, we present you with this document dated the 7th June, A.D.* 1965 *for your safe-keeping as a commemoration of this event.*

Signed Rev. Edwin Davies
Rev. M. R. Ellis.
Rev. D. J. Howells.
(*and members of the party*).

The Colonel was then presented with a copy of " History of Beddau ", by the author, Dillwyn Lewis, History Master at Bryn Celynnog Secondary School, Beddau. The party walked across the fields to the altar stone where it was inspected, and there a short service followed when Rev. M. R. Ellis commenced with Prayers. The Rev. D. J. Howells read the story of the Pentecost and the party of pilgrims sang " The Lord is My Shepherd " to the tune of Crimond. The blessing was given by Rev. Edwin Davies, Vicar of Llantrisant. The proceedings were recorded by BBC Wales Television who screened an edited version of the ceremony the same evening.

In Castellau Hamlet, approximately a mile outside Tonyrefail after passing Treferhyg Primary School, is Pantybrad (Hollow of Treason). This was once a hamlet of thatched cottages and boasted a nail factory owned by Morgan Evans, a candle factory and a flannel mill, nearby is Cae'r Efail reminding us that a smithy was located here. The name Pantybrad commemorates the capture of Edward II.

Edward of Caernarvon was born at Caernarvon Castle on 25th April, 1284 and ascended the throne in 1307. He inherited some difficult constitutional troubles and was not strong enough to impose his authority. Queen Isabella, his wife plotted against him and was helped by Roger Mortimer. Disaster came to this pathetic King from the intrigues of favourites, Caerphilly Despensers versus Hereford Mortimers. With the Mortimer soldiers at his heel, Edward fled to Glamorgan and wandered from Caerphilly until he finally pleaded sanctuary at Neath Abbey. Edward failed to recruit an army from Gower and on Sunday, 16th November he left the Abbey disguised as a monk, with a guide who was a spy.

There are many versions of the flight of King Edward II from his wife, Queen Isabella, and her supporters, but what may be the truth is that a Cistercian Monk from Neath guided the party to a Cistercian monastic establishment at Penrhys (Rhondda Valley) that while there refreshing themselves before proceeding to Llantrisant Castle the monk found an opportunity of communicating with spies and the spies intercepted the party somewhere on the ancient highway leading from the Rhondda to Llantrisant. The spot where the King was captured is still called "Pantybrad" (The Hollow of Treason). Hugh de Spencer was captured on Gwaun Miskin, east of Llantrisant and others of the King's company in the Park of Cloone on the south part of the hill where Llantrisant is built. The King and his friends were then taken to Llantrisant Castle. David ap Meurig and his fellow custodians may have been as much surprised as shocked when Henry of Lancaster knocked at the gate for admittance with a string of distinguished captives. The constable at this time, 1326, may have been Robert de Aston. He is referred to in a document as "sometime constable of Llantrisant and was very active in the year as taxer, collector and inquisitor".

The capture of King Edward is recorded in a document the original of which in Latin, is now at Lambeth Palace, London:—

> "*A.D.* 1326: *Eodem Anno XVI, Kalendas Decembris, vidilicet in Festa Sancti Edmundi Archiepiscopi, magna fuit, tempestas incipieus a media nocti, et duravit per totam diem, vidilicet tonibrua horriblia chorus cationis fuilgure pluvice et grandiois, cum ventis vehementious quasi inauditis. Et Eodem die Dominus Rex Edwardus fugiens in Wallium Wallensions fuit captus ductus ad Castellum Lantroisin propre Neiz, in Walliam.*

The Lamb and Flag Inn, Castellau, 1898
Watercolour by Mrs. L. Thomas, Llwyncrwn Uchaf Farm

The Lamb and Flag Inn, General View

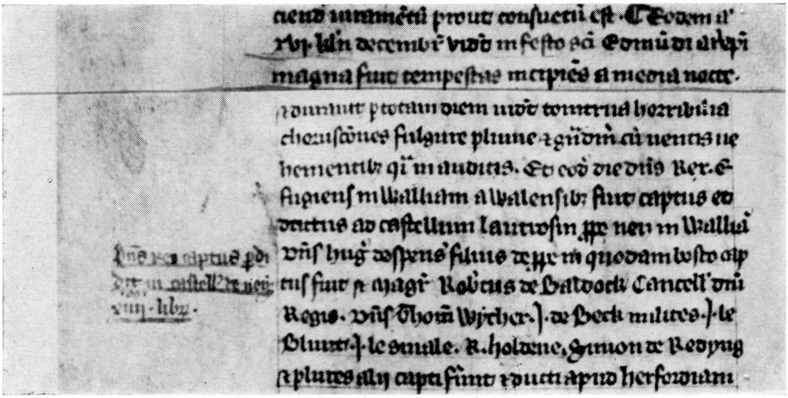

Facsimile of Document recording capture of Edward II at Pantybrad
By courtesy of Lambeth Palace

Plaque commemorating capture of Edward II, First English Prince of Wales near Tonyrefail

Darren Ddeusant — Druid's Altar Stone

The Independent Chapel, Castellau

Quaker's Meeting House, Treferig
(photograph taken late nineteenth century)

Castellau Fawr — 1974

Castellau Fawr in 1820

View of the Drawing Room, Castellau Fawr

View of the Adam Fire-place in the Drawing Room, Castellau Fawr

Dining Room, Castellau Fawr

Staircase, Castellau Fawr

Dominus Hugo Despenser, filius, de propre in quodam bosco captus fuit, and Magister Robertus de Baldock, Cancellarius domini Regis; Domini Thomas Wythers, T. de Beck, milites; T. le Smale, B. Holdene, Simon de Reading, et plurius alii capiti fuerunt et ducti apud. Herefordiam."

Translation: —

" The same year (1326) the 16th Kalends of December, that is to say, in the feast of St. Edmund, the Archbishop, a great storm arose in the middle of the night (15th) and continued the whole day of the (16th) with horrible thunder and lightning, rain and hail, accompanied by a vehement wind. The same day (16th) the Lord King Edward who was a fugitive in Wales, was captured by the Welsh and brought to the Castle of Llantrisant near Neath in Wales.

The Lord Hugh Despenser, the Younger, was captured close by, hiding in a small wood, also Robert de Baldock (Chancellor of the King); Lord Thomas Withers and John de Bek (Knights) J. le Bennet, J. le Smale, R. Holdene, Simon de Redynge, and numerous others were captured and taken to Hereford."

In this district was enacted the crowning tragedy of the reign of Edward II. Many traditions of the royal fugitive are preserved with a jealous care. B. H. Malkin in his "Antiquities of South Wales" states: —

" *It is said that the King in his own person was beloved by the Welsh and would have been safe in his retirement at Llantrisant, had he not trusted himself to the monk, in preference to their protection."*

The King was brutally murdered on 27th September, 1327 in Berkeley Castle a few months after his abdication; an object of compassion rather than hate, for folly not wickedness, brought about his end. Edward II is buried in Gloucester Cathedral.

For forty years, a marble tablet was set in the wall of an old thatched cottage at Pant y Brad, a hamlet near Tonyrefail. Just after World War II ended in 1945 the cottage fell into ruin and the tablet was lost. Later it was found intact by Mr. Edgar Llewelyn who was Headmaster at that time of Gellidawel County Secondary School. The tablet is now at Tonyrefail Comprehensive School.

Pant y Brâd
opposite on

Nov. 16th 1326, was captured
King Edward 2nd
(Edward of Caernarvon)

The guide of Captors was
Rev. Rhys Hywel (Rhys o'r Mynydd)
Nov. 16th 1909

The tablet was originally erected on 16th November, 1911, 585 years after the capture of Edward II (the first English Prince of Wales).

Near Pant-y-Brad stands the Manor House of Trefeurig (Treferig) which name translated into English means Manor of the Heath. The earliest traceable occupier of this Manor was Llewelyn ap Cynfrig who held large tracts of land in the area. However, with certainty the manor belonged to John ap Evan of Treferig who was born in 1585 and died 1630.

In 1646, John ap Jevan grandson of the fore-mentioned was born at Treferig. This man, later to be known as John Bevan, descendant of the Ancient British Kings and through his mother, Jane Dau, of Richard ap Evan of Collenna, descended from Plantagenet Kings, inherited the Manor and through the ways of the Heavenly King became Treferig's most famous occupant.

In his teens he was, in 1665, married to Barbara Awbrey, daughter of William Awbrey of Pencoed. She was about ten years his senior and a very devout lady of good birth. Bevan was an outspoken anti-tithe man and from the influence of George Fox, he became one of the leading Quakers of South Wales. He was excommunicated by the priest of Llantrisant Parish Church, whilst Barbara Bevan was present. This so affected her that she too became convinced and with her husband, became a zealous Quaker. John Bevan left a written account of himself (somewhere still extant) in which he wrote:—

> *"Sometime before the year* 1683, *we heard that our esteemed friend William Penn (also a Welshman) had a patent from King Charles the Second for the Province in America called Pennsylvania and my wife had a great intention to go thither and thought it might be good place to train up children amongst sober people and to prevent the corruption of them here."*

In July, 1683 he and his family sailed for America in the ship " Morning Star ", arriving in November and purchased 2,000 acres of land in Haverford West and Merion, in what is now North Philadelphia, the area was known as the Welsh Tract.

Whilst in America, he was a prominent man of affairs. He was chosen as a representative of the Provincial Assembly in 1687, 1693 and 1700, and was appointed a justice of Haverford, Philadelphia County in 1685 and for Chester County in 1689. In 1704 he finally returned home as he says " there was too much unpleasantness in Penn's country."

Bevan remained an anti-tithe man and after his return was, at the age of 83, for a short while imprisoned at Cardiff for this offence and for not attending Church.

Barbara his wife, died 26th November, 1710 aged 73 years and is buried in the Quaker cemetery near Treferig along with her husband who died in 1724. In his will (recorded at Llandaff) and proved 21st October, 1726, Bevan left Treferig to his grandson, John Bevan son of his eldest boy, Evan Bevan, who married Eleanor Wood of Darby near

Philadelphia. Edward Wolle now living in Cornwall is descended from his second child, Jane Bevan, who married Eleanor's brother John Wood.

The original members of the new meeting house were John Bevan (1636-1729) and his wife (1637-1710), Thomas Howell David, Howell Thomas, Lewis Richard, Merrick David and his wife, Watkin Thomas and John Richard.

In 1896, Thomas Allen Glenn in his book, " Merion in the Welsh Tract " states: —

> " *Two descendants of John Bevan now reside in the neighbourhood. One of them is Mr. John Bevan, a gentleman of independent means and advanced in years; and the other in female line. Mr. William John of Llantrissen town, who comes from Barbara said to have been the daughter of John Bevan Junior of Treferig who came from pennsylvania in* 1726-27 *to inherit the property after the death of his grandfather. This Barbara married a Mr. Davies and it is from their son, Rees Davies that Mr. John is descended.*"

In the Parish Church of Llantrisant, you can, with careful scrutiny find the tombstone of Jane, daughter of Richard ap Evan of Collenna Squire and also Richard Bevan, grandson of the John Bevan of Evan Bevan and Eleanor Wood. The tombstone of Jane, now used as a flagstone, can be found on the South Aisle, close to the pews, that of Richard is just beneath the altar steps (just under the carpet).

Amongst the various references to John Bevan, there seems to be some confusion about his marriage(s). However, family tradition has it that his first marriage was to Barbara Awbrey daughter of William Awbrey of Pencoed, Sheriff of Glamorgan. (My half-brother was christened Awbrey Bevan Wolle) Barbara Awbrey died 26th November, 1710 aged 73 years and 4 months. She married John Bevan, 1665 being nine years older than her husband. Bevan's second wife was Catherine (Awbrey?).

Of his children that remained in America, Jane and Evan married into an English Quaker family of Darby, Pennsylvania, Jane to John Wood, 1st October, 1687, and Evan to Eleanor Wood, 9th October, 1693. Eleanor had eight children, but today there are only two ladies alive bearing the name of that family of Bevan.

Jane's grand-daughter, Ann Wood married into a Scottish Protestant family by the name of Henry. Her husband William Henry, was cousin to the famous Virginian lawyer, Patrick Henry, who made that historical speech to the Virginia Assembly—" . . . as for me, give me liberty, or give me death ".

William Henry himself was a Colonel of the Lancaster, Pennsylvania militia of Washington's Continental Army. He was also an inventor and put the first steam boat on the river Delaware. In his twenties he befriended and became the patron of the artist Benjamin West, who eventually became the successor to Sir Joshua Reynolds as President of the Royal Academy of Arts.

Later in their lives, Ann and William Henry, attracted by the simplicity and sincerity of the Moravian Church, became members of that Church. Their son, William, who became a lawyer and High Court Judge, married a Moravian girl, Sabina Schropp, whose parents had originated from Germany. Their daughter Sabina Henry married into an influential Moravian family. Her husband John Frederick Wolle, was the son of a Moravian minister and missionary, and one of his brothers Peter, was a Bishop of the Church.

In 1926 a grandson of John and Sabina married a British Lady of Cornish descent, named Winifred Trewin. George Henry Wolle lived only three years after their son, Edward was born. These were tragic days for many, the great Wall Street crash of the late 1920's had ruined George Wolle, who apart from being an industrialist, was a member of the New York Stock Exchange. His whole fortune was lost and he died virtually penniless.

Winifred returned home to her sisters in England. The sisters were angels and their husbands, two brothers from the Lizard in Cornwall, bearing the name of Goodman helped to raise Winifred's youngest son.

Edward grew up among the war years and eventually went to sea. It was whilst serving as Second Mate in 1949, his ship dropped anchor in Falmouth harbour and here he met, and eventually married Sheila Polwin—a Cornish girl.

Having lived in England for the last twenty years, Sheila and Edward with their son Mark Polwin Wolle, now live in Cornwall, and there hope to settle.

This most interesting spot in the district of Castellau, the Quaker's Meeting House known locally as " Ty Cwrdd ", which is now in ruins, is situated among the trees near a stream. The walls are of dry local thin slate slabs skimmed with lime mortar. Before becoming derelict, the house had passed into private hands and used as a dwelling house. The best remembered inhabitant was William Williams, Ty Cwrdd. Members of his family still reside at Beddau. In 1820 the house was sold for £25 but in 1903 the house was bequeathed by the owner to the Society of Friends.

Edward recently visited the old Quaker meeting house at Treferig and the old cemetery there called Ty Cwrdd. Time has not dealt kindly with it and neglect has caused it all but to disappear. Quakers still own the land, but obviously do not care for it.

It is his fond hope to purchase Ty Cwrdd, to clear and rebuild it. Also to preserve the memory of John Bevan, son of the fifth Royal Tribe of Wales and descendant of the Great Caradoc, first Christian Prince of Britain, converted by Christ's own disciples.

A Tablet was erected on the existing gravestone in 1904 but is now lost. The Tablet stated:—

Here on the Ground Inherited by Him from
Iestyn ap Gwrgan
lie the remains of
John Bevan
Born in Glamorganshire, Wales 1686 died 1728
Judge of the Common Pleas and
Member of the Assembly at Pennsylvania
and of
Barbara Aubrey
his wife
Born 1687 died 1710
and of
Barbara, their daughter
died 1705 aged — years.

23. Penycoedcae

A mile and a half north of Beddau, lies the hamlet of Penycoedcae. Two hundred years ago, Penycoedcae was only a farm and part of the estate of Tir-Mab-Ellis. During the 1860's, Penycoedcae was a much bigger community than Beddau. The hamlet increased in population due to the Maritime Colliery, Pontypridd and the quarry near the village. The quarry was working in the 1920's. There was also a brick works at Penycoedcae and nearby were cottages called Brickyard Cottages. The cottages were also known, for a time, as Hewett's Town. The Hewetts Arms, now demolished, was over two hundred years old.

In 1967, Albert Coles, Esq., built an ultra modern residence on the site known as " Panorama " because of the wonderful views to be seen there. In 1971 the house was opened as a country club known as " The Beech Tree".

The most important house in Penycoedcae was Hill Male House, situated on the road to Pontypridd. The house was built in 1884 and was inhabited by Colonel Richard Hill-Male during the early years of this century. When he returned home from the South African War, a torchlight procession welcomed him. He was a solicitor by profession. An unusual feature of the house was a light fixed on top of the house which was used to assist visitors at night time. The light was so conspicuous that it could be seen for miles around and it often misled mariners sailing the Bristol Channel. It is said that Col. Hill-Male was paid a fee to stop using the light. The house has suffered the fate of so many large houses at the present time and is now only a reflection of its former splendour. During the 1960's the house was used as a business premises but in 1971 the building was renovated and is now a flourishing country club and motel. The house has been renamed Fawlty Towers after the popular television comedy show. Penycoedcae Church was built in 1875.

Lying near the road from Penycoedcae to Beddau is Tir-Mab-Ellis (Land of the son of Ellis). The house was built by a Mr. Ellis and is over two hundred years old. The house was the centre of a large estate and became the well-known residence of the Hewett family during the latter half of the nineteenth century. Plaques recording members of the family are to be found in Llantrisant Church.

24. Appendices

TRAHERNE OF COEDRIGLAN AND ST. HILARY, GLAMORGAN

Arms:

Argent, a chevron Sable between three ravens proper, two and one; on a canton barry of six argent and azure, a lion rampant gules.

Crest:

A goat's head erased surmounting a wreath.

Motto:

" Ofna Dduw a'r Brenhin " (Fear God and the King).

SEAL OF THE LLANTRISANT TOWN TRUST, 1889

The present Seal of the Llantrisant Town Trust was designed by Mr. Drane of Cardiff, and represents the arms of Consul de Clare and Despenser, families whose history in connection with the Borough is conterminous with that of Llantrisant.

The shield on the left is that of Despenser, quarterly 1 & 4 argent 2 & 3 gules, frette or, over all a bendlet sable. That in the centre is Clare, or three chevronels gules. On the right is that of Robert Consul, gules, 3 clarions. The silver mace of the Borough (which is of the year 1633) is shown inverted to indicate the extinction of the ancient corporation, as the torch at Roman funerals was reversed in token of death, but as liters scripta manet the quotation from Matthew ch. V. v. xiv: "A city that is set on an hill cannot be hid ".—" Dinas a osodir ar fryn ni ellir ei chuddio "—is singularly appropriate.

CHAIRMAN'S INSIGNIA

The Chairman's Jewel is of a silver gilt elongated shield base, double chamfered to the back edge, with a daffodil flower decoration at the apex, right angles, middle sides and base with a name-plate across the ribbon and letters in blue on white enamel. The Arms are cut out in silver gilt and mounted in relief.

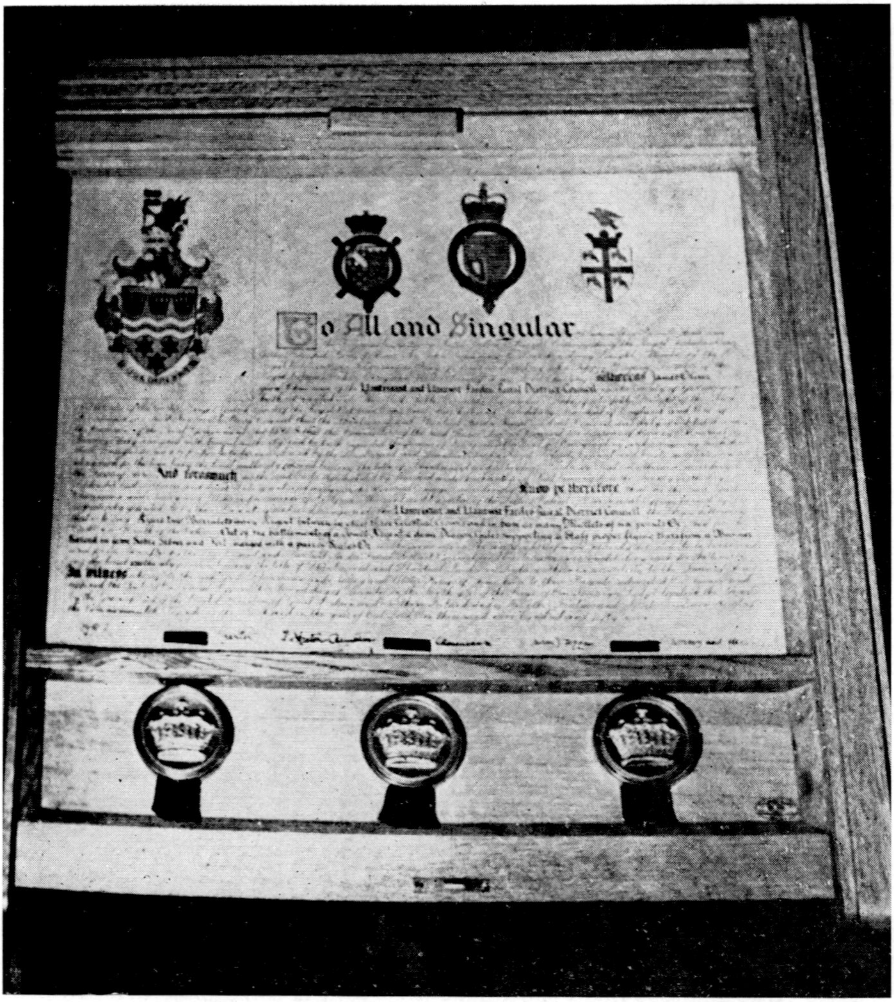
To All and Singular

DESIGN OF ARMORIAL BEARINGS
for the
LLANTRISANT AND LLANTWIT FARDRE RURAL DISTRICT COUNCIL, 1957

by H. Ellis Thomlinson, Heraldic Advisor to the R.D.C.A.

BLAZON

Arms:

Azure two bars wavy argent between in chief three celestial crowns and in base as many mullets of six points all or.

Crest:

On a wreath of the colours, out of the battlements of a tower argent a demidragon gules supporting a banner tierced in fesse sable argent and vert charged with a pair of scales or.

INTERPRETATION

Shield:

The shield expresses the location and constitution of the Rural District in heraldic terms. The two white waves represent the River Ely and the River Taff, which bound the District for much of its extent. The three golden celestial crowns, heraldic emblems indicative of religious connections, stand for the Parish of Llantrisant, named after SS. Illtyd, Gwynno and Tyfodwg. The three golden stars are for St. Illtyd who was a famous astronomer, and who is commemorated by stars in the arms of Dr. Williams's School, Dolgelley, and the Merioneth County Council, St. Illtyd's stars stand for Llantwit Fardre. These emblems are set against their appropriate background of blue.

Crest:

Above the shield is the closed helm proper to civic arms, with its crest-wreath and decorative mantling in the main colours of the shield, blue and white. Upon the wreath stands the crest. The base of the battlements of a tower, for Llantrisant Castle, recalling the long history of the former borough. From it rises the Red Dragon of Wales holding a banner in the same way as the Dragon in the Glamorgan County Council crest. The banner represents the industries and activities of the District. Its divisions of black, white and green represent coal-mining, limestone quarrying and agriculture; against this background a pair of gold scales represents the Treforest Industrial Estate, as it does in the Rhondda Borough Arms.

Motto:

The motto is that of Sir Brandon Rhys-Williams, Bt., of Miskin within the area; Llafur orfu bobpeth. Its Latin equivalent (Labor omnia vincit) is very popular in Civic Heraldry and is very appropriate in Welsh to this District, which is becoming more and more important industrially.

CHAIRMAN
LLANTRISANT PARISH COUNCIL

DESIGN OF THE CHAIRMAN'S INSIGNIA
for the
LLANTRISANT PARISH COUNCIL, 1967

Description:

(1) Surmounted by the "Black Prince's" helm and plume.

(2) The miner's lamp on a green background represents the coal taken from the green fields of Llantrisant, Tonyrefail and Gilfach Goch wards.

(3) The cross girdle in the national colours of Wales contains the three saintly crowns representing St. Illtyd, St. Gwynno and St. Dyffodwg, the three saints of the Parish Church of Llantrisant.

(4) The single flame represents cremation, and commemorates the first legal cremation in Great Britain carried out by Dr. William Price of Llantrisant at Caerlan in 1884. The Parish Council is the Burial Authority and the purple background denotes the mourning element.

(5) The three arrows at the foot of the medallion commemorate the prowess of the archers of Llantrisant at the Battles of Crécy and Agincourt.

The Badge was designed by Edward Gwyn Davies, Solicitor, Pontyclun and the work in drawing was executed by Mrs. J. Gwyn Checchi. Mr. Davies presented the Badge to the Council in 1967.

HIGH SHERIFFS FROM THE LLANTRISANT DISTRICT

1642	William Bassett of Miskin
1655	William Bassett of Miskin
1679	Thos. Gibbon, Esq., of Trecastle, Llanharry
1685	David Jenkins, Esq., of Hensol
1734	William Bassett, Esq., of Miskin
1735	Grant Gibbon Esq., Trecastle, Llanharry
1779	Christopher Bassett, Esq., of Lanelay
1785	Stephen White, Esq., of Miskin
1798	Samuel Richardson, Esq., of Hensol
1801	Llewellyn Traherne, Esq., of Castellau
1831	Richard Hoare Jenkins, Esq., of Llanharan House
1845	Robert Savours, Esq., of Trecastle, Llanharry
1849	Robert Boteler, Esq., of Llandough Castle & Maesmawr, Llantwit Fardre
1850	Rowland Fothergill, Esq., of Hensol Castle
1868	George Thos. Clark, Esq., of Talygarn, Pontyclun
1871	Vaughan Hanning Lee, Esq., of Lanelay
1882	Sir Joseph Layton Elmes Spearman, Baronet of Lanelay Hall
1897	Godfrey Lewis Clark, Esq., of Talygarn, Pontyclun

1921 Wyndham Damer Clark, Esq., of Talygarn, Pontyclun
1922 Sir Francis Caradoc Rose-Price, Baronet of Hensol Castle
1966 George Mervyn Williams, Esq., M.C., T.D., of Llanharan House
1969 Lieutenant-Colonel J. R. L. Traherne, of Castellau
1974 John Bevan, Esq., Crofta, Croesfaen, Llantrisant

QUAKERS' MEETING HOUSE

The following extracts from the Report published by the Charity Commissioners, dated 9th April, 1897 may be of interest.

" In this parish, near Treferig, there is a small tenement known as the Quakers' Meeting House, with a small cemetery attached. The house is now used as a dwelling-house, and has passed into private hands, but the cemetery still remains the property of the Society of Friends and is cared for by them, though not used now for the purpose of a burial ground.

There is no income arising from this trust.

The deeds in connection with this small property held by the Society of Friends do not include the title deeds of the property, but consist of the following.

1. Indenture, dated 14th February, 1750, made between John Bevan the elder, of Treferig, in the parish of Llantrisant, in the county of Glamorgan gent, Evan Bevan, John Bevan, the younger, and Richard Bevan, only sons and heirs at law of the said John Bevan the elder of the one part, and Nathanial Beadles, William Cooper, Ambrose Williams, John Jones, Thomas James, and Morgan Harry, of the other part, whereby it is witnessed that the said John Bevan the elder, Evan Bevan, John-Bevan the younger, and Richard Bevan, in consideration of *l*5 to them paid by the said parties or one of them, did, and each of them did give, grant, bargain, sell alien, release, enfeoff, and confirm unto the said Beadles, Cooper, Williams, Jones, James, and Harry, and to the survivor of them, and to the heirs and assigns of each survivor, all that one house commonly called or known by the name of the Quakers' Meeting House, one burial ground, one curtilage, one small garden, with all walls, fences, ways, lanes and privileges thereto belonging, with all singular their rights, members, appurtenances, which said granted premises are lying and being within the estate called Treferig aforesaid adjoining to the brook, with free and clear ingress, egress, and regress, to and from the said meeting house and premises by through or along such lanes, ways, and parks which then were or might be commonly made use of, to occupy the same or to or from the mansion house of Treferig aforesaid to hold unto the said Beadles, Cooper, Williams, Jones, James and Harry and to the survivor of them and to the heirs and assigns of such survivor for

ever, and it was thereby agreed and declared that all and every conveyance and assurance, and, should be and enure to the use and behoof of the said Beadles, Cooper, Williams, Jones and James, and Harry and to the survivor of them, and to the heirs and assigns of such survivor for ever.

2. A deed poll of the following day under the hands and seals of the said Nathaniel Beadles, William Cooper, Ambrose Williams, John Jones, Thomas James, and Morgan Harry, which after reciting the deed of the previous day continues:—

It is then made known and the said Nathaniel Beadles & do thereby signify, acknowledge, testify, and declare that the said grant and feoffment so made and confirmed unto them and to the survivor, and to the heirs and assigns of such survivor as aforesaid was only upon special trust and confidence in them reposed, that all and singular the said granted and enfeoffed premises should be to and for the sole use and privilege of the Society of people called Quakers, in manner and form following (that is to say) that the said meeting house burial ground, curtilage, and garden, with the appurtenances, should be used, occupied, and enjoyed by the said people called Quakers, to meet together in order to perform divine worship unto Almighty God according to that simplicity and innocency in spirit and in truth consistent with the Gospel Dispensation which they make a profession of, and to bury and inter their dead therein, and that they should suffer and permit them so to do as often or whenever they should or might have occasion to make that use of uses of the said premises or any part thereof for and during such time and times as the civil magistrates should permit and suffer them peacably to meet in to perform divine worship or to bury or to inter their dead. But from and after such time or times as they, the said people called Quakers, should or might be legally hindered, prevented, and not suffered by the civil magistrates to make those aforesaid uses thereof, that then and from thenceforth the said recited enfeoffed premises with the appurtenances should be to and for such other use of uses, intents or purposes whatsoever as they or the survivor of them or their heirs and assigns of such survivor should think most agreeable. And also upon trust that the last, three two or one survivors or survivor of them should or would within six months next after the decease of the rest of them, by good assurance and conveyance in the law from some valuable consideration well and sufficiently grant, release, assure, confirm, and convey over all and singular the said premises with the appurtenances unto some six or other number of persons to succeed as trustees, who should be named and appointed by the said people called Quakers at, in, and by appointment of their monthly or quarterly meetings of Friends of the county of Monmouth aforesaid, unto the heirs and assigns of such persons, they, the same persons, as new trustees, sealing and executing such deed of Declaration of Trust thereby repose in them as these presents (mutatis mutandis) or some such other deed or instrument in writing, duly executed as should seem meet.

3. Indenture of lease and release of various properties, dated September 1st and 2nd, 1785, which, after reciting the indenture of 14th February, 1750 declares that the said William Cooper, Ambrose Williams, John Jones, Thomas James, and Morgan Harry, were all respectively dead and that the Nathaniel Beadles, party to the abstracting presents, was the longest liver and survived all the rest of the said feoffees, and had thereby the fee and inheritance of, in, and to the premises in the said indenture of release in him vested, and that he did fully, clearly, and absolutely give, grant, bargain, sell, assign, remise, release, enfeoff, and for ever, quit, claim, and confirm the before-recited premises, & unto George Harford and others.

4. Indenture of lease and release, dated 28th and 29th December, 1838, which recites that George Harford, being the sole surviving trustee, had conveyed to Charles Lloyd Harford and others the burial ground aforesaid, but states that the meeting house had been sold previous to the date of those presents."

With reference to this sale, the minute book of the Monmouthshire Monthly Meeting of the Society of Friends, which body owned the meeting house and burial ground, contains the following minutes:—

> 10th December, 1820: "*It appearing to this meeting from an opinion taken by John Harford and now produced, that there is a power vested in the Society to dispose of the fee of Treferig Meeting House and Premises, and a person offering to purchase it as the sum of* 125, *John Harford is requested to treat with him on the subject, and to dispose of the same on the best terms he can obtain, but in such disposition the burial ground is to be reserved to the Society.*"
>
> 13th March, 1821: "*John Harford informs this meetings that he has made inquiries respecting the liability of Friends to the repairs of Treferig meeting house and premises, and has received a reply that as the Society has transferred all right to the premises they cannot be liable to any call upon that subject.*"

5. September 7th, 1848: Indenture of release and assignment by Charles Lloyd Harford and others to Edwin Napper and others.

6. April 16th, 1880: Indenture of release and assignment by Edwin Napper and others to Frederick Joseph Gibbon, of Neath and 13 other persons, who are (or the survivors of them) the present trustees.